Property Law Perspectives IV

Editors:
Dorothy Gruyaert
Eveline Ramaekers
Luke Rostill

Property Law Perspectives IV

intersentia

METRO

Ius Commune Europaeum

Intersentia Ltd
Sheraton House | Castle Park
Cambridge | CB3 0AX | United Kingdom
Tel.: +44 1223 370 170 | Fax: +44 1223 370 169
Email: mail@intersentia.co.uk
www.intersentia.com | www.intersentia.co.uk

Distribution for the UK and Ireland:
NBN International
Airport Business Centre, 10 Thornbury Road
Plymouth, PL6 7 PP
United Kingdom
Tel.: +44 1752 202 301 | Fax: +44 1752 202 331
Email: orders@nbninternational.com

Distribution for Europe and all other countries:
Intersentia Publishing nv
Groenstraat 31
2640 Mortsel
Belgium
Tel.: +32 3 680 15 50 | Fax: +32 3 658 71 21
Email: mail@intersentia.be

Distribution for the USA and Canada:
International Specialized Book Services
920 NE 58th Ave. Suite 300
Portland, OR 97213
USA
Tel.: +1 800 944 6190 (toll free) | Fax: +1 503 280 8832
Email: info@isbs.com

Property Law Perspectives IV

ISBN 978-1-78068-370-6
D/2016/7849/3
NUR 822

British Library Cataloguing in Publication Data. A catalogue record for this book is available from the British Library.

Dorothy Gruyaert
Eveline Ramaekers
Luke Rostill

PREFACE

1. Introduction

This book is the result of the fifth meeting of the Young Property Lawyers Forum (YPLF), which took place at Wadham College, Oxford, in September 2014. The YPLF is an informal network of junior property law researchers, which is primarily aimed at doctoral researchers but also includes researchers who obtained their doctorates within the last 5 years. The YPLF aims to bring property law scholars together from around the world and enable them to discuss their work with each other and with more experienced researchers. It provides an informal setting for young researchers to discuss innovative ideas and research in the area of property law, and to seek support in solving problems and improving their research. Property law is here taken in the widest sense of the term, encompassing fields such as EU property law, comparative property law, virtual property law, constitutional property law, environmental property law, property rights in land, water and volumes of space, and property law theory. As wide-ranging as these fields are, they all share a vision on how to give shape to the property law of the 21st century. Key to this vision is that property law is no longer confined to the borders of a single jurisdiction; that it is influenced by both legal and technological developments (e.g. in EU law, internet, social media, etc.); and that the interaction with other fields of law is crucial. The YPLF continues to form a network for property law researchers around the world with new conferences and publications for both junior and more advanced scholars. It is accompanied by this book series, *Property Law Perspectives* (PLP), in which the participants' papers are published. Past meetings of the YPLF have been held in Edinburgh (2009), Maastricht (2011), Stellenbosch (2012) and Leuven (2013). The latter three led to the publication of volumes I, II and III of *Property Law Perspectives*. The present volume, PLP IV, forms the most recent addition.

2. Renewed attention for the roots of property law

The papers presented at the YPLF are generally representative of the rapid developments currently taking place in property law and of the expansion of the field (or our understanding of it) to include aspects of environmental law, constitutional law, EU law, and internet law, to name a few. Nevertheless, the frontier research that many of the YPLF participants undertake still tends to be rooted in some of the oldest surviving doctrines of property law, with researchers either rediscovering these doctrines or reshaping them to adapt them to the present day context. The papers contained in the first three volumes of *Property Law Perspectives* reflect the novelty of the research conducted within the YPLF network. This volume, the newest addition to the series, shows that attention is also still being paid to the roots of property law. The papers contained within it take us on legal historical journeys, exploring basic principles and well-known concepts of property law such as the *prior tempore* rule and the rules on acquisitive and extinctive prescription. It seems fitting that these papers have resulted from the YPLF's meeting at a place so steeped in history as Oxford.

3. Contributions to this volume

The contributions to this volume deal predominantly with continental European legal systems, both those that form part of the present day French and German legal families as well as Roman law. Rafaël Ibarra Garza's paper, however, also takes us across the North Atlantic to the Mexican legal system.

The contribution by Ann Apers and Dorothy Gruyaert explores the tension between, on the one hand, retention of title clauses and, on the other hand, the rule on 'immovable incorporation' by which a movable object becomes incorporated into an immovable object such that it is no longer separately identifiable and therefore becomes part of the ownership of the immovable object. The rule on immovable incorporation clearly has the potential to defeat retention of title clauses. Apers's and Gruyaert's paper analyses in particular the new Belgian legislation, which at the time of writing is yet to be enacted, that deals with this issue and mitigates some of the risks for the party relying on the retention of title clause. At the same time, the paper draws parallels with the interpretation of the 'immovable incorporation' rule provided in Dutch and German law.

Elien Dewitte's contribution takes us into the world of the sale of churches. A decline in church attendance makes it difficult to bear the costs of heating, maintenance and restoration. Since demolition is often considered to be undesirable, selling the church is often the only way to ensure its continued existence. However, a sale often also means that the church will no longer be used for the purpose for which it was originally intended. The paper investigates how the use of either a long lease, a right of usufruct or a right of superficies can ensure that the new purposes to which the church is put after sale do not detract too much from its religious character.

Laurens de Hoog's paper takes us back to Roman law and to the beginnings of one of the most well-known and fundamental principles of property law, namely the *prior tempore potior iure* rule, by which property rights created earlier in time will generally defeat property rights created later in time. He explores the origins of this rule and how it applied to conflicts between security rights, between rights of use, and between security rights and use rights. By analysing the rule's origins he endeavours to aid our understanding of how and why the rule works nowadays.

Björn Hoops's paper investigates a case of excessive state action which is similar to expropriation in that it prejudicially affects a private party's property rights, but which differs from expropriation in the sense that the private party's property rights, although severely affected, are not taken away. Rather, the effect of the state action manifests itself such that there is a drastic reduction in the use the private party can make of its ownership. The case concerns a movable bridge in the municipality of Utrecht, the Netherlands, which was replaced by a non-movable bridge, thereby cutting off much of the river traffic crucial to the private company's business of ship building and repair. Hoops's paper analyses what, if any, legal basis there might be for a claim for compensation by the company. It does so by comparing Dutch and German law on the matter. In taking on this topic, which combines property law with constitutional law, Hoops follows a running theme throughout all of the PLP volumes, namely that of constitutional property law.

The contribution by Rafaël Ibarra Garza shows us how a concept of property law that had gone out of fashion can reappear, despite the fact that it had been replaced by new concepts and legal techniques. He explores the demise of the right of ownership as a method of securing an obligation in favour of other security devices, such as *pignus* (pledge) and *hypotecha* (hypothec/mortgage). This change in preference for security devices occurred already under Roman law, but now the use of the right of ownership to secure an obligation has reappeared in both Mexican and French contemporary law, even though the other security devices are well established. Ibarra Garza places this development in the context of what he calls the battle between legal technique and legal policy in the realm of securities and insolvency.

Johan Van de Voorde's paper provides us with a theoretical and historical analysis of the concepts of acquisitive and extinctive prescription. He compares both French and Belgian law on the subject. The paper focuses on the question of whether these two types of prescription should actually be seen as forming a unity, or whether there is still reason to treat them as two separate and distinct versions of prescription.

Oxford, Leuven, 2015

CONTENTS

Ann Apers
Dorothy Gruyaert

RETENTION OF TITLE v. IMMOVABLE INCORPORATION

1. Introduction

The retention of title is known as a strong security right because the holder remains the owner of the transferred assets until the underlying claim is fulfilled. However, the retained title is likely to be pushed aside when the assets are no longer identifiable in the purchaser's patrimony. Difficulties will arise in particular in the event that the assets sold under retention of title are incorporated into real property, *ie* attached to a real property in such a strong manner that they become part of that property. It is a basic principle of law that incorporation of a thing into a (real or personal) property, causes the owner of the main asset to gain ownership over the item incorporated into his property. Thus, the landowner acquires ownership over the newly incorporated item while the seller's retained right of ownership is compromised.

The new act on moveable security rights promulgated recently by the Belgian Parliament changed the impact of immovable incorporation on this security right severely in Belgian law. This inspired us to examine the interaction between a retention of title clause and the incorporation into real property of the sold items more thoroughly in this paper. We will start with a brief outline of the concept and legal consequences of the retention of title in Belgian as well as Dutch and French law. Subsequently, the impact made by immovable incorporation of the transferred assets will be discussed. The changes made to the effectiveness of a retention of title by the new Belgian act will be examined in the last chapter even though the act has not yet become effective.

2. Retention of title: concept and legal consequences

2.1. The reservation of ownership as security device

The legal arrangement of the retention of title entails the reservation of ownership in the assets to the seller until the price is fully paid, notwithstanding that the assets are already delivered to the buyer.[1] The transfer of ownership of the sold assets is thus postponed

1 Van Erp & Akkermans 2012, p. 475.

until the full payment of the purchase price. The seller remains owner in the meantime and is consequently granted a far-reaching protection in case of insolvency of the buyer.

The retention of title is an application of the right of ownership as security instrument and is widely accepted in European legal systems. In the Netherlands, retention of title is provided for by Article 3:92 of the Dutch Civil Code.[2] This article states explicitly that the agreement is considered to be entered into under a condition precedent of full satisfaction of that indebted performance. Also in France, the retention of title is regulated in the Civil Code, since the reform of the security rights in 2006 (Article 2367 CC).[3]

Under current Belgian law, the retention of title is stipulated in Article 101 of the Bankruptcy Act of 8 August 1997.[4] However, it is generally accepted by Belgian legal scholars that the retention of title also has proprietary effect in other cases of insolvency proceedings.[5] Nevertheless, in the judgment of 7 May 2010, the Belgian Cour de cassation rejected the third party effects of title retention in insolvency proceedings other than the seller's bankruptcy, in which it is expressly recognized in law.[6] This strict interpretation failed to gain approval in legal doctrine[7] and played an important role in the recent reform of Belgian law (*infra*, 3.1). It was held that Belgian law was put in a weak position in comparison with other European jurisdictions. The general third party effect of the retention of title had been widely accepted. In France, this was already recognized in the Act of 12 May 1980.[8] In the Netherlands, it was generally accepted under the unwritten

2 Art. 3:92, 1 NBW: "*Heeft een overeenkomst de strekking dat de een zich de eigendom van een zaak die in de macht van de ander wordt gebracht, voorbehoudt totdat een door de ander verschuldigde prestatie is voldaan, dan wordt hij vermoed zich te verbinden tot overdracht van de zaak aan de ander onder opschortende voorwaarde van voldoening van die prestatie.*"

3 Art. 2367 CC: "*La propriété d'un bien peut être retenue en garantie par l'effet d'une clause de réserve de propriété qui suspend l'effet translatif d'un contrat jusqu'au complet paiement de l'obligation qui en constitue la contrepartie. La propriété ainsi réservée est l'accessoire de la créance dont elle garantit le paiement.*" See also: Ordonnance n° 2006-346 du 23 mars 2006 relative aux sûretés, *JO* 24 mars 2006.

4 Art. 101 Faill.W.: "*Het faillissement doet geen afbreuk aan het recht van terugvordering van de eigenaar van de goederen die in het bezit zijn van de schuldenaar.*
Evenwel kunnen de roerende goederen, verkocht met een beding dat de eigendomsoverdracht opschort tot de volledige betaling van de prijs, slechts op grond van dat beding van de schuldenaar worden teruggevorderd, (voor zover dit schriftelijk is opgesteld) uiterlijk op het ogenblik van de levering van het goed. Daarenboven moeten die goederen zich in natura bij de schuldenaar bevinden. Ze mogen derhalve niet onroerend door incorporatie zijn geworden, noch vermengd zijn met een ander roerend goed."

5 Dirix 1998, p. 485, no. 13; Peeters 2002, p. 22, no. 10; Sagaert 2005, p. 59, no. 22.

6 Cour de Cassation 7 May 2010, www.cass.be, *Arr.Cass.* 2010, 1334, no. 321, *RW* 2011–12, 271, note M.E. Storme, *NjW* 2010, 502, note R. Fransis, *TBH* 2011, 550, note A. Gigot and *JLMB* 2012, 1242.

7 Bogaerts & Sagaert 2013, p. 3; Jansen & Sagaert 2012, p. 1371, no. 187; Storme 2012, p. 100, no. 9; Storme 2011, p. 254–266.

8 Loi n° 80-335 du 12 mai 1980 relative aux effets des clauses de réserve de propriété dans les contrats de vente. See also: Loi n° 85-98 du 25 janvier 1985 relative au redressement et à la liquidation judiciaires des entreprises and Loi n° 94-475 du 10 juin 1994 relative à la prévention et au traitement des difficultés des entreprises. See for a broader analysis: Laroche 2007, p. 105; Picod 2011, p. 461.

law.[9] In both jurisdictions, the general recognition of the retention of title was more recently embedded in the Civil Code (*supra*, 1.1).

2.2. *The legal positions under title retention*

2.2.1. Fiduciary relation

The retention of title is considered to be a clear example of ownership for security purposes (*fiducia cum creditore*). In that sense, ownership is more regarded as an instrument instead of a purpose on its own. In other words, the seller *functionally* retains a property security right.[10] However, it is often not considered as a property security right, because it is not granted but reserved.[11] Therefore, under current law, the ownership that is reserved is considered to be full ownership, and not merely a right of priority.[12] Ownership is not transferred, but retained. That is why retention of title is also a valid legal instrument under Dutch law, regardless of the ban on the fiduciary transfer of ownership (Article 3:84, 3 Dutch Civil Code).[13] The seller is simply reserving the right to recover his own property. However, the purchaser is also granted a proprietary protection. Both legal positions will be explained in what follows.

2.2.2. Position of the purchaser

Although the seller remains owner of the transferred assets, the right of the purchaser is more than a mere personal right against the seller. Retention of title is considered to be a transfer of ownership under a suspensive condition.[14] This means that the purchaser acquires a pre-emptive right of ownership (*Anwartschaftsrecht*).[15] As a consequence, the purchaser will be protected in case of insolvency of the seller. The purchaser remains in the position to acquire the ownership of the goods, by paying the outstanding amount of the purchase price.

An illustration of this can also be found at a European level. Article 7, paragraph 2 of the Insolvency Regulation (1346/2000) stipulates:

> *"The opening of insolvency proceedings against the seller of an asset, after delivery of the asset, shall not constitute grounds for rescinding or terminating the sale and* ***shall not prevent the***

9 See e.g.: Vriesendorp 1985, p. 22; Brahn 1988, p. 40 et seq. See also: Peter, Snijders, Janssen & Memelinck 2003, p. 174.

10 Van Erp & Akkermans 2012, p. 475. For *Belgium*: Dirix 1997, p. 484, no. 10. For *the Netherlands*: Brahn, 1988, p. 184; Verstijlen 2006, p. 1186, no. 41. For *France*: Barrière 2004, p. 311; Laroche 2007, p. 108.

11 Van Erp & Akkermans 2012, p. 505.

12 See also: Van Erp & Akkermans, 2012, p. 476.

13 See Brahn 1988, p. 48 *et seq.*

14 For *the Netherlands*, see: Asser 2010, p. 523; Scheltema 2013, p. 156; Verstijlen 2006, p. 1186, no. 41.

15 *Germany*: Baur, Baur and Stürner 2009, p. 843, no. 59.32 et seq.; See also: Van Erp & Akkermans 2012, p. 301.

***purchaser from acquiring title** where at the time of the opening of proceedings the asset sold is situated within the territory of a Member State other than the State of the opening of proceedings.*"

2.2.3. Position of the seller

The seller remains the owner of the delivered assets until the purchase price is fully paid.[16] He enjoys a strong position in case of insolvency of the buyer.[17] The sold assets remain out of the insolvent patrimony if the buyer becomes insolvent before having paid the full purchase price.[18] That is why retention of title is called the "*queen of the security rights*".[19]

However, a retention of title does not grant absolute security to the seller: the buyer may have transformed the sold assets, if the sale agreement relates to the manufacturing process, or the buyer may have proceeded with a sub-sale.[20] To assert the right of retention of title, it is required that the assets are still identifiable in the estate of the buyer. This brings us to the next point: the difficulty of exercising a retention of title in case of the incorporation of the assets.

3. Relation between retention of title and incorporation

3.1. Principles of immovable incorporation

The main research question of this contribution is how a retained title is affected after its object is transformed through immovable incorporation. Incorporation entails the attachment of a movable item (or personal property) to an immovable (or real) property, usually land or a building.[21] A physical incorporation of movables into an immovable has two legal consequences.[22] Firstly, the classification of the movables will change after incorporation. They will lose their movable classification and become immovable themselves.[23] Secondly, the ownership rights will be affected by the incorporation. The physically attached item will legally become a part of the immovable and will seize to

16 For *the Netherlands*: Reehuis 2013, p. 45, no. 50.

17 *Belgium*: Dirix 2011, p. 14. *France*: Bourassin, Brémond & Jobard-Bachellier 2010, p. 331; Picod 2011, p. 461. *The Netherlands*: Asser 2010, p. 539; Reehuis & Heisterkamp 2012, p. 701; Verstijlen 2006, p. 1186, no. 41.

18 For *the Netherlands*: Reehuis 2013, p. 90, no. 90. See also Van Erp & Akkermans 2012, p. 475.

19 Stoufflet 1983, p. 320, no. 2.

20 Van Erp & Akkermans 2012, p. 472. For an example in *French law*, see: Cass.fr. 9 January 1990, *D.* 1991, 130, note G. Virassamy.

21 This contribution compares jurisdictions (France, Belgium and the Netherlands) which use the civil law terminology of movable ('*meuble*' in French – '*roerend*' in Dutch) and immovable ('*immeuble*' in French – '*onroerend*' in Dutch). We will therefore use the terms movable and immovable instead of the common law terms personal and real property.

22 Van Vliet 2002, p. 70; Bouly 2014, p. 112.

23 In *France* and *Belgium* this is implied in art. 518 of the respective Civil Codes. In *the Netherlands* the idea can be found both in art. 3:3 NBW (which gives a definition of immovable property) and 3:4 NBW (which gives the definition of component parts).

exist as an autonomous object of rights. The ownership right over the former movable will disappear while the ownership right over the immovable will extend to the newly incorporated thing.[24] The change at the level of the ownership rights is called 'accession'. Accession is therefore one of the consequences of immovable incorporation, the other being a change of classification.

As said, retention of title constitutes the reservation of an ownership right over a sold item. If this item is incorporated into an immovable, accession will occur and the ownership on the item will disappear.[25] The seller who loses his reserved title, will become a creditor.[26] Since it is the physical attachment, the incorporation, that causes the seller to lose his title, it is important to know under which circumstances property is considered immovable through incorporation.

3.2. *Criteria for immovable incorporation: France, Belgium and the Netherlands*

3.2.1. France

In France, the term 'incorporation' is not defined in any legal provision, but the Supreme Court[27] introduced a criterion in 1974 which is still in use today. According to this ruling, an object will only be classified as immovable when an attachment, anchorage or foundation exists proving that the item is not simply resting on the ground by its weight.[28] The requirement of a physical bond between the movable and the immovable is thus

24 *France* and *Belgium*: Article 552 of the Civil Code. *The Netherlands*: Articles 5:20 NBW and 5:3 j° 3:4. In Dutch doctrine the relationship between Articles 3:3 and 3:4 NBW is debated. More specifically, it is unclear whether a thing classified as immovable based on Article 3:3 automatically becomes a component element in the sense of Article 3:4 NBW. Since both lead to the loss of ownership on the incorporated item, either through Article 5:20 or 5:3 NBW, we will not go into this discussion in this contribution. For further analysis, see amongst others Mak 2002, p. 12–13; Wolfert 2003a, p. 191–197; Wolfert 2003b, p. 279–285; Van Maanen 2006, p. 228–230; Heyman & Bartels 2006, p. 270–275; Hoofs 2012, p. 89.

25 In French and Belgian law, the rules on accession are not deemed imperative law (French Cour de Cassation November 6 1970, *D.* 1971, 395). French case law and doctrine regard the renouncement by the land owner of his ownership right over the incorporated asset, as a solution for the seller who wants to sell under retention of title knowing the object will be physically attached to the land. (French Cour de Cassation May 29 2001, *RTDciv* 2001, 93; Revet 2006, p. 351). This nonetheless causes new problems and uncertainties such as whether publicity is required, whether an ownership right can exist of the object that is not factually identifiable, etc. See Apers & Gruyaert, 2015, *to be published*. In Dutch law, the rules on accession are imperative. Articles 5:3 and 5:20 NBW both state "… as far as the law does not determines otherwise", leaving no space for contractual arrangements (other than the right of superficies described in Article 5:101 NBW). Therefore, a clause in which the land owner renounces his ownership right after incorporation cannot prevent accession and the consequent loss of title for the seller. (On immovable constituent elements: Reehuis 2013, p. 38–41).

26 *Belgium*: Article 554 CC; Sagaert 2003, p. 776.

27 *Cour de Cassation* in French.

28 Cour de Cassation June 10 1974, *Bull.civ.* 1974, IV, 146, no. 183; Strickler 2006, p. 53–54; Libchaber 2009, p. 30–31.

interpreted in a rather strict sense in French law. Cabins[29] and mobile homes,[30] for example, will not be considered immovable even if they remain in place and are equipped with utilities such as electricity and plumbing. The seller who reserves ownership over an item which is later attached to the land in a loose manner will not lose his title because the property will not be classified as immovable and accession will not occur.

Two provisions seem to refine the idea that movables incorporated into land or a building become immovable themselves and accede to that land or building, which causes the seller to lose his title. Articles 2370 CC[31] and L 624–16 *Code de Commerce*[32] both state that a reserved title survives incorporation of its object if the object can be removed without damage. The question arises how these articles relate to the strict incorporation criterion. Would it be possible for an object to become immovable through incorporation yet remain detachable without damage? If so, certain objects would become immovable without acceding to the land and sellers would be able to recover ("revindicate") these items after they become immovable. French scholars seem to agree that a category of immovables that can be detached without damage does not exist.[33] The application of the criterion for incorporation will lead to the same result as the criterion used in Articles 2370 CC and L 624–16 Code de Commerce: a reserved title over a movable attached firmly to an immovable will disappear and revindication will no longer be possible.[34]

We can conclude that under French law a seller only loses his title when the object of the sale is firmly attached to the land.

3.2.2. Belgium

Although the Belgian legal provisions on accession and the immovable classification of things are identical to the French, the current interpretation of the term 'immovable' differs

29 Court of Appeal Orléans March 16 2009, no. 08/00333, www.dalloz.fr.

30 Cour de Cassation April 28 1993, *Bull.civ.* 1993, no. 56, *JCP G* 1993, II, 315, no. 2203, obs. H. Périnet-Marquet. Remarkably, the French government argued in a case before the European Court of Justice that caravans were immovable and therefore exempt from VAT under Article 2 of Directive 77/388. The European Commission did not agree and brought the case before the ECJ, which ruled in favour of the Commission. (Commission v France (C-60/96) [1997] E.C.R. I-3827. For a more thorough comment: Ramaekers 2014, p. 452–453.

31 Article 2370 CC: "*L'incorporation d'un meuble faisant l'objet d'une réserve de propriété à un autre bien ne fait pas obstacle aux droits dus créancier lorsque ces biens peuvent être détachés sans subir de dommage.*" (The incorporation of a movable object, of a title retention, into another property does not impede the rights of the creditor when the items can be detached without damage – own translation.).

32 Article L 264–16 Code de Commerce: "*La revendication en nature peut s'exercer dans les mêmes conditions sur les biens mobiliers incorporés dans un autre bien lorsque la séparation de ces biens peut être effectuée sans qu'ils en subissent un dommage.*" (The revindication in kind is possible under the same circumstances for movables incorporated into another item if the separation of these objects is possible witout them suffering damage – own translation.).

33 Crocq 1999, p. 444; Mainguy 2000, p. 69; Crocq 2007, no. 85; De Lambertye-Autrand 2007, no. 79. *Contra*: Aynès & Crocq 2008, p. 356, fn. 52.

34 Crocq 2007, no. 88.

widely in both jurisdictions. Under Belgian law, a movable originally only became immovable through incorporation if it was attached to the land through foundations. Later, the impossibility to separate an object attached to land or a building from that land or building without damage was considered necessary but sufficient for the object to lose its movable classification.[35] In 1988, the Belgian Supreme Court[36] relaxed the requirement of a strong physical connection. Gas station pumps were classified as immovable in a decision in which the court equated buildings with objects that are "durably and usually connected or attached to the land".[37] Authors interpreted the case as creating a new criterion for immovables, for which the technical possibility for the item to be removed no longer prevented an immovable classification.[38] In 2008, the court opened up the category of immovables even further. In a decision concerning harbour cranes, the court decided that limited, functional movements do not deprive an object which stays in the same place and is attached to the land, of its classification as immovable property.[39] An item can thus move in a limited, functional manner and still be considered immovable through incorporation under Belgian law. Because of this broad interpretation, the category of immovables is much wider in Belgium than in France. A seller under title retention runs a higher risk in Belgium of seeing the sold item become immovable and to lose his title due to accession.

3.2.3. The Netherlands

The Dutch civil code contains two articles based on which the movable classification of an asset changes to an immovable one.[40] The first provision is Article 3:3 NBW, which describes immovables. Listed in Article 3:3 NBW are the soil, minerals that have not yet been extracted, plants that are attached to the soil, and buildings and constructions that are durably united with the land, either immediately or through connection with other buildings or constructions. The last category of buildings and constructions is comparable to the French and Belgian category of immovables through incorporation in that a physical connection between an item and the land or a building is required for the item to acquire an immovable classification. In 1997 the Dutch *Hoge Raad* explained how the durable connection requirement in Article 3:3 NBW should be interpreted in its landmark *Portacabin* case. According to the *Hoge Raad*, an object is united with the land durably when it is destined through its nature and design ("*bestemd naar aard en inrichting*") to stay in place durably, even though the item could be removed theoretically

35 See for example: Court of Appeal Brussels December 24 1898, *Pas.* 1899, II, 138; Court of Appeal Ghent July juli 1904, *Pas.* 1905, II, 301; Court of Appeal Liège January 21 1932, *Pas.* 1932, II, 212; Court of Appeal Ghent May 17 1966, *Rev.fisc.* 1967, 322; Duranton 1841, 45, no. 105; Kluyskens 1940, 14, no. 7; De Page & Dekkers 1975, 604, no. 640.

36 French: *Cour de Cassation* and Dutch: *Hof van Cassatie.*

37 Cour de Cassation September 15 1988, *TBBR* 1990, 211, case comment J. Kokelenberg.

38 Kokelenberg 1990, p. 216; Tilleman 2005, p. 6.; Sagaert 28, p. 457.

39 Cour de Cassation February 14 2008, *Fisc.Koer.* 2008, afl. 8, 464, case comment P. Souffriau, *Fiscoloog* 2008, afl. 1120, 18 (weergave CB), www.cass.be (12 maart 2008), *JLMB* 2008, afl. 38, 1700, case comment E. Van Brustem, *Pas.* 2008, afl. 2, 440, *RCJB* 2010, afl. 1, 53, case comment J. Romain, *RW* 2008–09, afl. 11, 456, case comment V. Sagaert, *TBBR* 2009, afl. 7, 387, *TBO* 2008, afl. 3, 118, case comment M. Muylle.

40 Van Vliet 2002, p. 73.

speaking. The intention of the builder, to the extent that it is cognizable, should be taken into account to determine the destination to keep the object in place. This destination has to be knowable for third parties.[41] If the intention to keep an item in place sufficed for it to become immovable, the category of immovables could potentially become very broad. In the 1997 decision, the *Hoge Raad* already emphasised that the intention of the builder and the destination of the object must be knowable to third parties in order to have an impact on the classification. Later case law confirmed that only an objective destination can be taken into account for the classification of an immovable, while a purely subjective intention of the owner is deemed irrelevant.[42] Nonetheless, the use in case law of the Portacabin criteria lead to a very broad interpretation of the term 'immovable'.[43]

The second provision causing a movable to become immovable is Article 3:4 NBW. This article describes the criteria for an asset to become a constituent element, i.e. a part, of another asset. If an item is considered to be a constituent element, it will follow the main asset's regime. One of the aspects of that regime is the classification. If a movable becomes a constituent element of an immovable, it becomes immovable itself.[44] An object can become part of another in two ways. According to the first paragraph of Article 3:4 NBW a constituent element of an object is anything considered part of it according to common opinion ("*verkeersopvatting*"). The public notion requirement refers to the generally common notion that two or more assets are connected to each other to such an extent that they form one property.[45] Factory machines, for example, can be constituent elements of a factory building if the building and the machines are constructed in accordance with one another and the building can be considered unfinished without the machines.[46] The second paragraph of Article 3:4 NBW adds a physical criterion to the intellectual one used in the first paragraph. If an object cannot be removed from a building without serious damage, the object is a constituent element of the building.

A movable that becomes immovable, will accede to the land or building under Dutch law, regardless of whether the change in classification stems from Article 3:3 or 3:4 NBW (*supra*, footnote 24). Since immobilisation can occur on two grounds, with the former

41 Hoge Raad October 31 1997, *NJ* 1998, 97.

42 See for example on railway testing constructions: Hoge Raad May 13 2005, *BNB* 2005, 2446, no. 212; on a caravan: Hoge Raad June 26 2005, *BNB* 2005, 275, *VN* 2005/33.28, *FED* 2005, 107, *NTFR* 2005, 862, *BB* 2005, 853; Van Vliet 2002, p. 69.

43 See for example Hoge Raad June 7 2002, *BB* 2002, 806, *BNB* 2002, 283, *FED* 2002, 354, *NTFR* 2002, 836, *PW* 2002, 21494, *VN* 2002, 32.22, *WFR* 2002, 902; Hoge Raad October 25 2002, *BB* 2003, 765, *JOL* 2002, 564, *NJ* 2003, 241, *PW* 2003, 21597, *RvdW* 2002, 170; Hoge Raad June 6 2003, *BB* 2003, 815, *BNB* 2003, 271, *BR* 2003, 819, *FED* 2003, 330, *GST* 2003, 186, *JOR* 2003, 222, *NTFR* 2003, 1015, *PW* 2003, 21611, *VN* 2003/34.16; Heyman 2000, p. 118; Janssen 2006, p. 867. On the similarities in the expansion of the term 'immovable' in Dutch and Belgian law, see Apers 2014, p. 189–194.

44 Strictly speaking, the object that becomes part of another legal object does not have a classification of its own as it has lost its legal independence. The object shares in the classification of the main object.

45 Mijnssen & De Haan 2001, p. 51–52; Reehuis & Heisterkamp 2012, p. 7; Snijders & Rank-Berenschot 2012, p. 28.

46 Hoge Raad November 15 1991, *NJ* 1993, 1154, no. 316.

provision being interpreted very broadly, a Dutch seller under retention of title runs a higher risk of losing his title than his French colleague. Items that will not be considered immovable under French law can sometimes be classified in Dutch law as immovable, causing the seller to lose his title and become a mere creditor.

4. Recent intervention in Belgian law: Act on moveable security rights

4.1. Scope of application

The act of 11 July 2013 on moveable security rights brought some changes with regard to the retention of title.[47] The new act provides a general recognition of the retention of title by embedding it in the Civil Code.[48] The legislator meets the objection raised in the aftermath of the judgment of the Court of Cassation that limited the scope of the retention of title to the cases of bankruptcy (*supra*, 1.1). The general recognition of the retention of title in the French and Dutch legal systems served as inspiration for the Belgian law makers. The retention of title will be effective not only when the seller is in state of bankruptcy, but in *all* insolvency proceedings.

The new Act also remedies the fact that the effectiveness of the retention of title under current Belgian law is limited to sale agreements, in terms of Article 101 of the Bankruptcy act.[49] Article 69, para. 3 of the new act stipulates that the retention of title can be enforced, regardless of the legal classification of the agreement which it is part of. This means that a clause of title retention which was inserted in a manufacturing agreement will have third party effect. The validity of a retention of title clause in contracts other than sale contracts is also accepted in French law[50] and Dutch law.[51] Of course, the retention of title is still limited to the claim the payment of which it secures. 'All money' retention of title clauses are still impossible under Belgian law.[52] Only the range of secured claims is broadened.

4.2. No requirement of publicity

The new Belgian act still requires a written document that is formulated at the latest at the moment of delivery of the assets (Article 69, para 1 new act). Also in French law, the

47 Wet van 11 juli 2013 tot wijziging van het Burgerlijk Wetboek wat de zakelijke zekerheden op roerende goederen betreft en tot opheffing van diverse bepalingen ter zake, *BS* 2 augustus 2013. This act has not yet become effective. It should come into force at the latest on 1 January 2017 (see Article 109 of the new act).

48 See also: Derijcke 2013, p. 718, no. 125; Dirix 2013, p. 39, no. 68; Jansen 2014, p. 147, no. 12.

49 See for the parliamentary proceedings: *Parl.St.* Kamer 2012–2013, no. 2463/003 and no. 2463/005, www.dekamer.be.

50 Calme 2011, p. 50.

51 Article 3:92 (2) NBW. See: Asser 2010, p. 523, no. 522; Hartkamp 1988, p. 85; Reehuis 2013, p. 11, no. 12.

52 The same is true, to a large extent for French and Dutch law. Extended title retention clauses can be effective in German and English law. For an elaboration on this point, see: Van Erp & Akkermans 2012, p. 480–484.

retention of title is only effective if the formal requirement of a written document is fulfilled (Article 2368 CC). The Belgian legislator added that if the purchaser is a consumer, his explicit consent should be clear (Article 69, para 2 new act). The Dutch legal system adheres to the consensual nature of the retention of title agreement, which means that there are no formal requirements.[53]

However, the retention of title does not require registration. That is the case in the current state of Belgian law, and was upheld in the new Act. Whether or not the retention of title should be registered was discussed during the parliamentary proceedings. The contrast with the registered pledge was raised, but the legislator nevertheless decided that registration was not required. The main reason was that also in the French and Dutch legal systems, the proprietary effects of the retention of title are recognized without the requirement of publicity.[54] Although registration is still not required, the new Act does provide the possibility to register the retention of title clause in the new pledge register. This registration will appear to be highly recommended in case the sold asset would be incorporated in another good.

4.3. *Remedy in case of incorporation: Article 71*

The soon enough former Article 101 of the Belgian Bankruptcy Act allowed the seller under title retention to recover the asset in case of insolvency on the condition that the asset could be found in kind ("*in natura*") in the estate of the buyer. As mentioned before, incorporation leads to an object becoming part of another object and therefore acceding to it. After incorporation, the object no longer exists in kind excluding recovery by the seller under retention of title.

The new Belgian act relaxed the in-kind requirement. With regard to movables incorporated into immovables, the future Article 71, Title XVII of Book III BW states that a retained title continues to exist even if the object has been incorporated into an immovable on the condition that the title was registered. This is an exception to the idea that retention of title does not require registration (*supra*, 3.2).

The question arises how this new provision should be interpreted. What will be the exact position of the seller, especially with regard to execution of his right. The act itself is not clear on this, neither are the explanatory documents. Certain authors apply the provisions organising the position of the pledger by analogy. The reason seems to be that both the act and the explanatory documents often treat a seller under retention of title and a pledger similarly.[55] For the survival of a retained title after incorporation, no clear reference is made to the position of the pledger. However, according to this view, the rule that a pledger who sees the object of his right incorporated, will have priority over the

53 See: Reehuis, 2013, p. 5, no. 5; Van Erp & Akkermans 2012, p. 475.
54 See also: Jansen 2014, p. 148, no. 15.
55 See for example future Article 70, Title XVII, Book III BW.

proceeds in case of a sale,[56] also applies for the seller.[57] Strictly speaking, the seller will no longer be the owner of the incorporated object. Instead, he becomes a creditor who has preference over the proceeds of a sale, limited to the value of the object of his title.[58] Execution will have to take place over the entire asset in which the object of his right was incorporated.[59]

Because execution over the entire immovable might have detrimental effects on the business of the owner, as well as on the rights of a mortgagee,[60] other authors defend a different view. In this interpretation a factual distinction needs to be made. If the item is truly incorporated, meaning that removal of the object would cause serious damage, the above rules will apply. Recovery is not possible and the seller becomes a preferential creditor. However, if the item classified as immovable through incorporation can be removed without damage, revindication should be possible.[61] The reasons to defend this view are diverse. Allowing recovery when the item can be removed prevents a forced sale of the entire immovable, thus allowing the business of the landowner to continue.[62] Beneficial for the seller is that he will be able to avoid a conflict with the mortgagee.[63] Furthermore, a movable charge is usually faster and less expensive. Finally, the distinction offers a partial solution for the unwished-for effects of the Belgian *Cour de Cassation*'s broad interpretation of the term 'immovable'.[64]

With this view, a discrepancy would arise between the criterion for a change in classification on the one hand, and the criterion for accession on the other. The criterion for an immovable classification would still be the broad formula used by the *Cour de Cassation* (*supra*, 2.2.2). The criterion for accession of an object sold under retention of title, however, would be the possibility to be removed without damage, which resembles the stricter criterion used by the French *Cour de Cassation* (*supra*, 2.2.1). An object could lose its movable classification to become immovable without losing its autonomous existence as an object of right. Simply stated: a movable could become immovable without acceding. This would constitute a new form of horizontal division of ownership in Belgian law, next to condominium ownership and the right of *superficies*.[65]

Whether the Belgian courts will follow this view, remains to be seen as the act has yet to come into force.

56 Future art. 19, Title XVII, Book III BW.

57 Bogaerts & Sagaert 2013, p. 2–3; Cataruzza 2013, p. 193; Georges 2013, p. 357–358.

58 Memorie van Toelichting, *Parl.St. Kamer* 2012–13, no. 2463/001, p. 44.

59 Sagaert 2015, p. X, no. 32.

60 According to the explanatory documents the seller who registered his title will take priority over the mortgagee, even if the latter holds a title that was registered first: Memorie van Toelichting, *Parl.St. Kamer* 2012–13, no. 2463/001, p. 70–71. This position is described as a 'superpriority'.

61 Jansen 2014, p. 162–163; Sagaert 2015, p. X, no. 32.

62 Apers & Gruyaert 2015, to be published.

63 Sagaert 2015, p. X, no. 32.

64 On those effects: Sagaert 2008, p. 458–459; Bouly 2014, p. 111–130.

65 Apers & Gruyaert 2015, to be published.

5. Conclusion

Traditionally, the incorporation of an item sold under retention of title into an immovable property causes the seller to lose his title. In the Netherlands and Belgium especially this effect of incorporation is problematic since both jurisdictions use very broad interpretation of immovables through incorporation. The new Belgian act on movable securities remedies the risk for the seller. A retained title can now survive incorporation. Nevertheless, the exact effects of the new provisions are not clear yet. One interpretation could be to distinguish between whether or not the object can be removed without damage. In this view, the Belgian rules on retention of title after incorporation would lean more towards the French approach than the Dutch, offering a better protection for the seller who retains ownership for security purposes.

Bibliography

Apers 2014
A. Apers, "Party Autonomy in the Classification of Things", in B. Akkermans, E. Marais and E. Ramaekers (eds.), *Property Law Perspectives II*, Cambridge, Intersentia, 2014, 185–204.

Apers & Gruyaert 2015
A. Apers and D. Gruyaert, "Eigendomsvoorbehoud en onroerende incorporatie volgens de nieuwe pandwet: welk nieuws onder de zon?", *Tijdschrift voor Privaatrecht* 2015, *to be published.*

Asser 2010
C. Asser, A.I.M. van Mierlo and A.A. van Velten, *Vermogensrecht algemeen: Zekerheidsrechten* in *Asser-serie*, 3, Deventer, Kluwer, 2010, 626 p.

Aynès & Crocq 2008
L. Aynès and P. Crocq, *Les sûretés: La publicité foncière*, Paris, Defrénois, 2008, 386 p.

Baur, Baur & Stürner 2009
F. Baur, J. Baur and R. Stürner, *Sachenrecht*, München, Beck, 2009, 1086 p.

Barrière 2004
F. Barrière, La *réception du trust au travers de la fiducie* in *Bibliothèque de droit de l'entreprise*, 66, Parijs, Litec, 2004, 604 p.

Bogaerts & Sagaert 2013
S. Bogaerts and V. Sagaert, "Nieuwe Pandwet: grondige hervorming van zekerheden op roerende goederen", *Balans* 2013, no. 700, 1–4.

Bouly 2014
S. Bouly, "Does the expansion of the concept 'immovable' influence immovable accession?', in B. Akkermans, E. Marais and E. Ramaekers (eds.), *Property Law Perspectives II*, Cambridge, Intersentia, 2014, 111–130.

Bourassin, Brémond & Jobard-Bachellier 2010
M. Bourassin, V. Brémond and M.-J. Jobard-Bachellier, *Droit des sûretés*, Parijs, Dalloz, 2010, 733 p.

Brahn 1988
O.K. Brahn, *Fiduciaire overdracht, stille verpanding en eigendomsvoorbehoud naar huidig en komend recht* in *Studiepockets privaatrecht*, Zwolle, Tjeenk Willink, 1988, 222 p.

Calme 2011
S. Calme, *La réserve de propriété de droit français et de droit allemand dans le contexte européen*, Frankfurt am Main, Peter Lang, 2011, 206 p.

Cattaruzza 2013
J. Cattaruzza, "Les grands axes de la réforme des sûretés mobilières", *Bank. Fin.R.* 2013, 183–194.

Crocq 1999
P. Crocq, "Réserve de propriété et contrat d'entreprise: inefficacité de la clause de renonciation à l'accession immobilière et généralité de la condition d'existence en nature de bien revendiqué", (case comment on Cour de Cassation March 2 1999), *RTDciv* 1999, 442–445.

Crocq 2007
P. Crocq, "Sûretés mobilières - Clause de réserve de propriété", *JurisClasseur Civil Code* 2007, 47 p.

de Lambertye-Autrand 2007
M.-C. de Lambertye-Autrand, "Classification tripartite des immeubles - Immeubles par nature", *JurisClasseur* 2007, 1–30.

De Page & Dekkers 1975
H. De Page and R. Dekkers, *Traité élémentaire de droit civil belge*, V, Brussel, Bruylant, 1975, 1167 p.

Derijcke 2013
W. Derijcke, "La réforme des sûretés réelles mobilières", *TBH* 2013, 691–722.

Dirix 1997
E. Dirix, "Eigendomsvoorbehoud", *RW* 1997–1998, 481–496.

Dirix 2011
E. Dirix, "Artikel 101 Faill. W." in *Voorrechten en hypotheken. Artikelsgewijze commentaar met overzicht van rechtspraak en rechtsleer*, Mechelen, Kluwer, 2011.

Dirix 2013
E. Dirix, *De hervorming van de roerende zakelijke zekerheden*, Mechelen, Kluwer, 2013, 317 p.

Duranton 1841
A. Duranton, *Cours de droit français suivant le code civil. Tome II*, Brussel, Société Belge de Librairie Hauman et C°, 1841, 532 p.

Georges 2012
F. Georges, "La réforme des sûretés mobilières", *Rev. Dr. ULg.* 2013, 319–368.

Hartkamp 1988
A.S. Hartkamp, *Compendium van het vermogensrecht voor de rechtspraktijk*, Deventer, Kluwer, 1988, 389 p.

Heyman 2000
H.W. Heyman, "Wanneer is een gebouw of werk 'duurzaam met de grond verenigd'?" in S.E. Bartels and M.J. Milo (eds.), *Open normen in het goederenrecht*, Den Haag, Boom Juridische Uitgevers, 2000, 91–122.

Heyman & Bartels 2006
H.W. Heyman and S.E. Bartels, "Is een huis een bestanddeel van de grond? Een rechtsgeleerde dialoog tussen H.W. Heyman en S.E. Bartels", *NTBR* 2006, vol. 7, 270–275.

Hoofs 2012
K. Hoofs, *Doorbreking van de natrekking in rechtsvergelijkend perspectief*, Nijmegen, Wolf Legal Publishers, 2012, 309 p.

Jansen & Sagaert 2012
R. Jansen and V. Sagaert, "Overzicht van rechtspraak. Zakelijke zekerheden (2004–2010)", *TPR* 2012, 1223–1399.

Jansen 2014
R. Jansen, "Eigendomsvoorbehoud", in J. Baeck and M. Kruithof, *Het nieuwe zekerheidsrecht*, Antwerp, Intersentia, 2014, 139–166.

Janssen 2006
J.F.M. Janssen, "De uitleg die wordt gegeven aan de artt. 3:3 lid 1 en 5:20 sub e BW, ontregelt de zaak", WPNR 2006, 855–867.

Kluyskens 1940
A. Kluyskens, *Beginselen van Belgisch burgerlijk recht - Zakenrecht*, Antwerpen, Standaard, 1940, 392 p.

Kokelenberg 1990
J. Kokelenberg, "Onroerend van nature, een begrip in beweging?", (case comment to Court of Cassation September 15 1988), *TBBR* 1990, 215–218.

Laroche 2007
M. Laroche, *Revendication et propriété: du droit des procédures collectives au droit des biens*, Parijs, Defrénois, 2007, 373 p.

Libchaber 2009
R. Libchaber, "Biens", *Rép. civ. Dalloz* 2009, 1–46.

Mainguy 2000
D. Mainguy, "La question de l'opposabilité d'une clause de réserve de propriété affectant des biens incorporés à un immeuble", *Recueil Dalloz* 2000, 69.

Mak 2002
E. Mak, "Roerend of onroerend? Een onderzoek naar de goederenrechtelijke kwalificatie van telecomkabels", *AA* 2002, vol. 1, 6–14.

Mijnssen & De Haan 2001
F.H.J. Mijnssen and P. De Haan, *Goederenrecht: Algemeen goederenrecht*, in *Asser-serie*, 3, Deventer, W.E.J. Tjeenk Willink, 2001, 540 p.

Nève 2000
P.L. Nève, *Eigendomsvoorbehoud* in *Nederlandse Vereniging voor Rechtsvergelijking*, 60, Deventer, Kluwer, 2000, 1–89.

Peter, Snijders, Janssen & Memelinck
J. Peter, H. Snijders, J. Janssen and P. Memelinck, "Goederenrecht" in X., "Enkele belangrijke uitspraken van de Hoge Raad der Nederlanden. Overzicht van rechtspraak (1997–2001)", *TPR* 2003, 166–207.

Ramaekers 2014
E. Ramaekers, "Classification of objects by the European Court of Justice: movable immovables and tangible intangibles", *European Law Review* 2014, p. 447–469.

Reehuis 2013
W.H.M. Reehuis, *Eigendomsvoorbehoud* in *Monografieën BW*, Deventer, Kluwer, 2013, 119 p.

Reehuis & Heisterkamp 2012
W.H.M. Reehuis and A.H.T. Heisterkamp, *Goederenrecht*, in *Pitlo*, 3, Deventer, Kluwer, 2012, 806 p.

Revet 2006
T. Revet, "Même non publiée, la clause de renonciation à l'accession immobilière est opposable au liquidateur judiciaire ès qualité de représentant des créanciers" (case comment to Cour de Cassation March 29 2006), *RTDciv* 2006, 351–354.

Peeters 2002
I. Peeters, "Eigendom tot zekerheid" in E. Dirix and A. Cuypers (eds.), *Voorrechten en hypotheken. Artikelsgewijze commentaar met overzicht van rechtspraak en rechtsleer*, 1, Mechelen, Kluwer, 2002, afl. 24, 1–74.

Picod 2011
Y. Picod, *Droit des sûretés*, Parijs, P.U.F., 2011, 528 p.

Sagaert 2003
V. Sagaert, "Het "in natura"-vereiste bij eigendomsvoorbehoud: de gevolgen van bewerking, vermenging en wederverkoop" (case comment to Brussels November 19 2002), *TBH* 2003, 773–781.

Sagaert 2005
V. Sagaert, "Nieuwe perspectieven op het eigendomsrecht na twee eeuwen burgerlijk wetboek" in P. Lecocq, B. Tilleman and A. Verbeke (eds.), *Zakenrecht/Droit des biens*, Brugge, Die Keure, 2005, 43–85.

Sagaert 2008
V. Sagaert, "Onroerendmaking door incorporatie: over het verschil tussen beweegbaarheid en verplaatsbaarheid", (case comment to Court of Cassation February 14 2008), *RW* 2008, vol. 11, 457–459

Sagaert 2015
V. Sagaert, "Het eigendomsvoorbehoud onder de Pandwet", *to be published*

Snijders & Rank-Berenschot 2012
H.J. Snijders and E.B. Rank-Berenschot, *Goederenrecht*, Deventer, Kluwer, 2012, 651 p.

Storme 2011
M.E. Storme, "Eigendomsvoorbehoud en samenloop buiten faillissement", *RW* 2011–12, 254–266.

Storme 2012
M.E. Storme, "Actualia roerende zakelijke zekerheden" in M.E. Storme (ed.), *Insolventie- en beslagrecht*, Brugge, die Keure, 2012, 95–155.

Stoufflet 1983
J. Stoufflet, "L'usage de la propriété à des fins de garantie" in A. Bruyneel and A.M. Stranart (eds.), *Les sûretés (sûretés traditionnelles, réelles et personnelles, en droit français et en droit belge; sûretés issues de la pratique; droit international privé): colloque de Bruxelles des 20 et 21 octobre 1983),* Brussel, Feduci, 1983, 319–343.

Strickler 2006
Y. Strickler, *Les biens*, Parijs, P.U.F., 2006, 536 p.

Scheltema 2013
A.H. Scheltema, "Eigendomsvoorbehoud, overdracht en verpanding van eigendom onder opschortende voorwaarden", *MvV* 2013, 155–164.

Tilleman 2005
B. Tilleman, "De notie roerend en onroerend goed" in P. Lecocq, B. Tilleman and A. Verbeke (eds.), *Zakenrecht*, Brugge, die Keure, 2005, 3–42.

Van Erp & Akkermans 2012
S. Van Erp and B. Akkermans (eds.), *Cases, Materials and Text on Property Law* in *Ius Commune Casebooks*, Oxford, Hart Publishing, 2012, 1170 p.

Van Maanen 2006
G. Van Maanen, "Is een gebouw bestanddeel van de grond?", *NTBR* 2006, vol. 6, 228–230.

Van Vliet 2002
L.P.W. van Vliet, "Accession of Movables to Land: I", *EdinLR* 2002, 67–84.

Verstijlen 2006
F. Verstijlen, "Paritas creditorum, voorrang en preferentie", *TPR* 2006, 1157–1236.

Vriesendorp 1985
R.D. Vriesendorp, *Het eigendomsvoorbehoud* in *Serie recht en praktijk*, Deventer, Kluwer, 1985, 142 p.

Wolfert 2003a
E.C.M. Wolfert, "Bestanddeel of zaak? Over het onderscheid en de samenhang tussen de artikelen 3:4 en 5:20 BW (I)", *WPNR* 2003, 191–197.

Wolfert 2003b
E.C.M. Wolfert, "Bestanddeel of zaak? Over het onderscheid en de samenhang tussen de artikelen 3:4 en 5:20 BW (II)", *WPNR* 2003, 279–285.

Elien Dewitte

(ALTERNATIVES TO) THE SALE OF CHURCHES

1. Introduction

For some time now, the problem of unoccupied churches has been high on the political agenda. Authorities all over Europe ring the alarm bell: the decline in church attendance makes it hard to bear the costs of maintenance, heating and restoration of the churches. Demolishing a church, however, can only be a last resort, considering the emotional value that is coupled with the building. Selling the building remains often the only, but also a quite radical solution: it means the end of using the building for the goal it was established for. Therefore, when confronted with a church that is no longer frequented, the following questions arise: how can we balance, on the one hand, the use of the church for religious worship and, on the other hand, other uses of the church that yield more income? And, if a church is to be sold, how can the seller be protected against uses of the church that would be contrary to the religious character of the building?

Property law can offer an answer to the abovementioned questions. In this paper, we will first consider whether a church can count as a public land good or not. Next, we deal with alternatives to the sale of a church through the establishment of rights of long lease, usufruct and superficies. Finally, we will consider, when a church nevertheless would be sold, what clause can adapt a sale to its specific subject, that is a church. However, this paper focuses on the Property law-related questions on the topic in Belgian law, with some comparison with French and Dutch law, but omits the questions related to canon, administrative and tax law.

2. Preceding determination: the church as public land good

First and foremost, we have to verify whether a given church can count as public land. Public land goods are those goods that are meant for everyone's use by virtue of their nature or a decision of the government, or that are included in the public land through an act.[1] A broader and more modern criterion says that it contains all goods that, due to a

1 *Belgium*: Cass. 9 March 1950, *Arr.Cass.*, 1950, p. 457; Cass. 3 May 1968, *RW*, 1968–69, p. 409; Cass. 18 May 2007, *TBO*, 2008, p. 9, note Van Heuven, *NjW*, 2007, p. 652, note Rasschaert, *RW*, 2007–08,

particular adaptation, historic or scientific interest, are necessary for a public service and which in that function cannot be replaced by another good.[2] Churches meant for public utility and belonging to provinces, municipalities or fabric committees are included in the public land.[3] Private chapels, convent churches and presbyteries, on the other hand, do not count as public land.[4] The reason it is important whether a church counts as a public land good is that such goods cannot be subjects of commerce unless the government grants a change of use (*desaffectatie*).[5] Before such a change of use has been approved, the church cannot be sold and no property rights can be established on it.[6]

However, Belgian law contains an exception to the required change of use for the Flemish government,[7] the provinces[8] and the municipalities.[9] Besides these exceptions determined by decree, the Belgian Court de Cassation introduced an additional one: in a judgement of 18 May 2007 the Court recognized the admissibility of the establishment of an independent right of superficies on a public land good if it does not obstruct the public purpose of that good.[10] Whereas the classic view argues for an *in abstracto*

p. 736, note Sagaert and *Rev.not.b.*, 2007, p. 631, note Lagasse. *France*: Public land goods are those goods which are meant for everyone's use or for a public service (Malaurie 2003, p. 52, nr. 167).

2 Waline 1936, p. 523.

3 *Belgium*: Cass. 3 February 1860, *Pas.*, 1860, I, p. 121; Cass. 11 November 1886, *Pas.*, 1886, I, p. 401; Cass. 6 November 1940, *Pas.*, 1940, I, p. 279; Liège 6 April 1939, *Pas.*, 1940, II, p. 6. *France*: In the same sense: Malaurie 2003, p. 51, note 56.

4 Cass. 28 March 1878, *Pas.*, 1878, I, p. 149 (presbytery); Brussels 14 May 1938, *Pas.*, 1938, II, p. 113; Brussels 28 June 1948, *JL*, 1948–49, 97 (presbytery); Rb. Aarlen 22 November 1989, *JT*, 1991, p. 480, note Godding (presbytery).

5 *Belgium*: Cass. 25 September 2000, *Arr.Cass.*, 2000, p. 1428 and *RW*, 2002–03, 775: '*dat de goederen van het openbaar domein, aangezien ze tot eenieders gebruik bestemd zijn, buiten de handel vallen en niemand, bij overeenkomst of door usucapio op die goederen een privaat recht kan verwerven dat genoemd gebruik zou kunnen belemmeren en afbreuk doen aan het recht van de openbare overheid om het te allen tijde volgens de behoeften en het belang van alle burgers te regelen en te wijzigen*' (free translation: 'that public land goods, while they are meant for everyone's use, are not subjects of commerce and nobody, through an agreement or through *usucapio* can obtain a private right on those goods that the mentioned use could hinder and could harm the right of the public government to regulate and alter it at any time according to the needs and the interest of all citizens'). *France*: In the same sense: Malaurie 2003, p.52, nr. 167.

6 Sagaert 2014, p. 129, nr. 153.

7 Article 10 Decree 18 July 2003 on Public Private Partnership, *BS*, 19 July 2003, 46.497: '*... zakelijke rechten vestigen op de onroerende goederen die behoren tot het openbaar domein, voorzover de gevestigde zakelijke rechten niet kennelijk onverenigbaar zijn met de bestemming van deze goederen*' (free translation: '... establish property rights on immovables belonging to public land, as far as on the condition that the established property rights are not clearly incompatible with the purpose of those goods').

8 Article 185 Decree 9 December 2005, *BS*, 29 December 2005, p. 56.891.

9 Article 191 Decree 15 July 2005, *BS*, 31 August 2005, p. 38.153.

10 Cass. 18 May 2007, *RW*, 2007–08, p. 736, note Sagaert, *NjW*, 2007, p. 652, note Rasschaert, *Rev.not.b.*, 2007, p. 631, note Lagasse and *TBO*, 2008, p. 9, note Van Heuven: '*voor zover een privaat recht van opstal de bestemming [tot het gebruik van allen] niet verhindert, het kan worden gevestigd op een goed van het openbare domein*' (free translation: 'as far as a private right of superficies the purpose [for everyone's use] not hinders, it can be established on a public land good').

exclusion of the establishment of property rights on public land, the aforementioned judgement indicates an evaluation *in concreto* of the question whether the right of long lease is compatible with the public purpose of the land and the use by everyone. Moreover, it seems that decision also applies to other property rights, as it is the case in France,[11] although legal uncertainty remains in the absence of a Belgian judgment in that sense.[12]

When the government has granted a change of use of the church (classic view), one has to verify which property right meets the best the desires and wishes of the parties concerned. It is also possible that one has to evaluate which property right is compatible with the purpose of the church to be used by everyone (modern view). In the following part, we deal successively with the right of long lease, the right of usufruct and the right of superficies.

3. Alternatives to the sale of churches

3.1. Right of long lease

3.1.1. Definition and application cases

First of all, parties can use a right of long lease as an alternative to the sale of a church. A right of long lease is a property right for the use and enjoyment of an immovable property subject to the payment of a periodic fee, the ground rent (Article 1 Belgian Long Lease Act[13]). The right of long lease contains the most comprehensive right of use and enjoyment on another man's immovable property.[14] For instance, the long leaseholder has a comprehensive right of use and enjoyment on the buildings, the land and the subsoil, while the right of superficies is merely oriented at the construction of buildings.[15] Besides, the right of long lease can refer to a building as well as to a part of a building.[16] Further, the deed has to be registered at the mortgage registry office with a view for the right of long lease to have effect against third parties in good faith with a competing right (Article 1, second paragraph Belgian Long Lease Act).[17]

11 For a *bail emphytéotique*: Article L1311-2 *Code général des collectivités territoriales*, and for the establishment of property rights: Article L2122-20 *Code général de la propriété des personnes publiques*.

12 Sagaert 2014, p. 134–135, nr. 156.

13 Act 10 January 1824 on the right of long lease, *BS*, 10 January 1824.

14 Sagaert 2014, p. 551, nr. 684.

15 Sagaert 2014, p. 620, nr. 785.

16 Deli 1998, p. 40, nr. 9; Derine, Van Neste & Vandenberghe 1984, p. 853, nr. 1000A; Van Oevelen 1990, p. 9, nr. 4.

17 Deli 1998, p. 55, nr. 53; Dekkers & Dirix 2005, p. 293, nr. 739; De Page 1953, p. 607, nr. 714, 1°; Hansenne 1996, p. 1234, nr. 1221*bis*; Kluyskens 1953, p. 244, nr. 239; Mostin 2004, p. 94, nr. 41; Sagaert 2014, p. 566, nr. 701; Vandenberghe & Viaene 2006, p. 44, nr. 36; Van Oevelen 1992, p. 328, nr. 5; Verstappen 2004, p. 7, nr. 11.

Nowadays, a right of long lease is sometimes used for the installation of solar panels on the roof of a church by someone other than the owner of the church. In that case, the right of long lease is established on that part of the roof of the church where the solar panels will be placed, so that the owner of the church still can fully dispose of the rest of the roof and of the immovable.[18] But considering the comprehensive competences of the right holder, a right of long lease can also be established on the whole church with a view to its exploitation as a hotel, concert hall, shop etc. Further, that right can also be used as an alternative to classic financing. When the owner of the church has liquidity problems, he can transfer the bare ownership by way of security to a person (X) with reservation of a right of long lease. The purchase price then serves as the financing source, while the ground rent comprises the repayment and the interest. In that way, the original owner of the church preserves the use and enjoyment of his immovable, while X has the best security, namely a *'tréfonds'*, that can become a full ownership in case of insolvency of the long leaseholder.[19] Finally, the local authority can take a church on a long lease, for instance because of the importance of the church as a characteristic building for the city-skyline, and, through the insertion in the contract of a clause in that sense, bear the heavy costs of the restoration or renovation of the building.[20]

3.1.2. Duration

When establishing a right of long lease parties have to bear in mind that it is essentially a temporary right: the duration of it is limited between 27 (18 in France[21]) and 99 years (Article 2 Belgian Long Lease Act). In Dutch law however, parties are free to determine the duration of their right of long lease (Article 5:86 Dutch Civil Code): even a perpetual right is possible, whereas that is unthinkable under Belgian or French law. That legal minimum and maximum duration is in Belgium at least of imperative law,[22] and – according to the majority opinion – even of public order.[23] Non-observance of the legal minimum and maximum duration will lead to conversion, i.e. the use of the classification which bears the closest resemblance to the classification aspired to by the parties.[24] So when the solar panels-project ends earlier than after twenty-seven years, parties run the risk that the agreement of long lease will be converted in a lease,[25] with negative financial

18 *Belgium*: Vandorpe & Haverbeke 2010, p. 5. *France*: Ravanas 2009, nr. 19.

19 Sagaert 2014, p. 555, nr. 688; Snaet 2008, p. 71, nr. 40.

20 Timmermans 2011, p. 1066, nr. 664.

21 *Bail à construction*: Article L251-1 *Code de la construction et de l'habitation*; *bail emphytéotique*: Article L451-1 *Code rural et de la pêche maritime.*

22 Bergen 4 May 1998, *JLMB*, 1999, p. 444 and *Rec.gén.enr.not.*, 2000, p. 146; Deli 1998, p. 44, nr. 22; Hansenne 1996, p. 1232, nr. 1219; Mostin 2004, p. 73, nr. 2 and p. 82, nr. 19.

23 Ghent 16 March 1972, *RW*, 1971-72, p. 1986; De Page 1953, p. 595, nr. 699; Derine, Van Neste & Vandenberghe 1984, p. 852, nr. 999; Van Oevelen 1992, p. 346, nr. 20.

24 Sagaert 2014, p. 556, nr. 690.

25 *Belgium*: Deli 1998, p. 44, nr. 22; de Montpellier 2003, p. 15, nr. 29; Derine, Van Neste & Vandenberghe 1984, p. 855, nr. 1000C; Hansenne 1996, p. 1232, nr. 1219; Laurent 1887, p. 448, nr. 368; Mostin 2004, p. 82, nr. 20 and p. 83, nr. 21; Verstappen 2004, p. 18, nr. 34.

and fiscal consequences.[26] Such conversion will also take place if one of the parties had the right to end the agreement of long lease ex parte before the period of twenty-seven years has passed.[27] However, parties are allowed to put an end to the agreement of long lease by mutual agreement, even before the expiration of the minimal duration of twenty-seven years unless the termination was at one with the establishment of the right of long lease.[28] Moreover, the Belgian Court de Cassation decided in a judgement of 30 March 2006 that a right of long lease can be terminated before the expiration of the minimal duration in the event of an insolvency procedure or dissolution of a legal person-long leaseholder and that an automatic conversion into lease was in this case not under discussion.[29] When, on the contrary, a right of long lease is established for a duration that is longer than ninety-nine years, the duration will be limited up to ninety-nine years,[30] which is the maximum duration for every property right of use and enjoyment.[31] A stipulation in the agreement through which the long leaseholder has the right at the end of the maximum duration of ninety-nine years to extend unilaterally the agreement or to renew it for a new period of ninety-nine years will be considered as unwritten.[32] However, it is possible to insert a stipulation with the obligation for the parties to negotiate in good faith during the last year of the long lease on a possible renewal of the long lease and its terms, i.e. on the establishment of a new property right.[33]

3.1.3. Remuneration

Also necessary under Belgian (Article 1 Belgian Long Lease Act) and French law[34] is the *ground rent*. That fee has to be periodic[35] and a once-only fee seems thus impossible, although the payment of a non-recurrent real fee in combination with an annual symbolic fee can offer a way out.[36] The obligation for the long leaseholder to pay a ground rent was originally aimed at the prevention of a doubt arising as time goes by on the question who is in fact the owner, a fear that has disappeared as a result of the introduction of the

26 Vandorpe & Haverbeke 2010, p. 5.

27 Deli 1998, p. 45, nr. 23; Derine, Van Neste & Vandenberghe 1984, p. 855, nr. 1000C; Van Oevelen 1992, p. 347, nr. 20.

28 Sagaert 2014, p. 582, nr. 728. In the same sense: Muylle 2012, p. 198–199, nr. 265.

29 Cass. 30 March 2006, *Arr.Cass.*, 2006, p. 740, *RW*, 2006–07, p. 678, note Vanhove, *T.Not.*, 2008, 97 and *TBBR*, 2008, p. 88, note Waterkeyn.

30 Deli 1998, p. 44, nr. 22; de Montpellier 2003, p. 15, nr. 29; Derine, Van Neste & Vandenberghe 1984, p. 855, nr. 1000C; Hansenne 1996, p. 1232, nr. 1219; Laurent 1887, p. 448, nr. 368; Mostin 2004, p. 82, nr. 20 and 84, nr. 23; Van Oevelen 1992, p. 327, nr. 4.

31 Sagaert 2014, p. 557, nr. 692.

32 Ghent 16 March 1972, *RW*, 1971–72, p. 1986; Rb. Dendermonde 4 July 1942, *T.Not.*, 1942, p. 139.

33 Sagaert 2014, p. 558, nr. 693.

34 Terré & Simler 2010, p. 820, nr. 932 and p. 821, nr. 934. For a *bail à construction*: Article L251–5 *Code de la construction et de l'habitation*; Bergel, Bruschi & Cimamonti 2009, p. 335, nr. 292.

35 Although Article 1 Belgian Superficies-Act indicates an annual fee, also another periodicity seems possible, for instance monthly, quarterly, biennial etc. (Deli 1998, p. 51, nr. 42; Mostin 2004, p. 109, nr. 77; Sagaert 2014, p. 573, nr. 713).

36 Carton de Tournai & Charlier 1971, p. 71; Deli 1998, p. 51, nr. 42; Donnay 1974, p. 220, nr. 11. *Contra* Van Oevelen 1992, p. 349, nr. 21.

Mortgage Act. So, a symbolic fee is possible, although a real fee for the right of use and enjoyment is nowadays the most common in the real estate practice.[37] Parties also have to pay attention to the fact that, in the absence of an indexing clause, the same nominal ground rent will be due (even if the right is established for the longest duration possible, namely 99 years!).[38] Moreover, the long leaseholder will only be released from the obligation to pay the ground rent if he was deprived of his enjoyment of the immovable during five consecutive years (Article 11 Belgian Long Lease Act). However, parties are free to deviate from this by contract: it is for instance possible to stipulate that even from the first day that it is impossible to exercise the right of use, no ground rent will be due.[39]

The situation is different under Dutch law. There, the obligation for the right holder to pay a ground rent is only a possibility, and according to the Civil Code, that fee does not need to have a periodical character (Article 5:85, paragraph 2 Dutch Civil Code). Moreover, such a fee can be symbolic as well as real.[40]

3.1.4. Rights and obligations of the long leaseholder

Through the establishment of a right of long lease the holder is given the largest rights of use and enjoyment; he can set up constructions or plantings on the immovable property on which the right of long lease is established (Article 5, third paragraph Belgian Long Lease Act, Article 5:89, paragraph 3 Dutch Civil Code). And what's more, when the right of long lease has the character of a French *bail à construction*, the right holder is even obliged to build.[41] Moreover, during his right of long lease, the holder remains owner of the buildings that he erected[42], so there arises an accessory right of superficies pursuant to the agreement of long lease[43] that is linked to the duration of the right of long lease (and thus with a maximum of 99 years),[44] contrary to the 50 years-maximum duration of an independent right of superficies in Belgium.[45]

The long leaseholder has a larger right of enjoyment than the usufructuary: he can change the purpose of the good, he has no obligation of guarantee or inventory, his right

37 *Belgium*: Carton de Tournai & Charlier 1971, p. 71; Deli 1998, p. 50, nr. 39; de Montpellier 2003, p. 17, nr. 34; Derine, Van Neste & Vandenberghe 1984, p. 872–873, nr. 1006; Sagaert 2014, p. 561, nr. 696; Snaet 2008, p. 54, nr. 13; Van Oevelen 1992, p. 333, nr. 9. *France*: A symbolic fee is also possible for a *bail à construction* (Bergel, Bruschi & Cimamonti 2009, 335, nr. 292).

38 Sagaert 2014, p. 574, nr. 714.

39 Sagaert 2014, p. 575, nr. 714.

40 De Jong & Ploeger 2008, p. 39, nr. 22.

41 Article L251-1 *Code de la construction et de l'habitation*.

42 *Belgium*: Derine, Van Neste & Vandenberghe 1984, p. 866, nr. 1004C; Donnay 1974, p. 225, nr. 16; Mostin 2004, p. 103, nr. 56; Snaet 2008, p. 56, nr. 14; Van Oevelen 1992, p. 330, nr. 7. *France*: Terré & Simler 2010, p. 821, nr. 934 and p. 823, nr. 937 (*bail à construction*).

43 Ghent 29 May 1895, *Pas.*, 1895, II, p. 414; Ghent 25 May 1901, *Pas.*, 1901, II, p. 334; Hansenne 1996, p. 1236, nr. 1227; Lecocq 2000, p. 143.

44 De Page 1953, p. 606, nr. 713.

45 De Page 1953, p. 606, nr. 713; Donnay 1974, p. 225, nr. 16; Werdefroy 1983, p. 326, nr. 16.

of long lease is not personal, and the regulation of the expiration of his right in the event of him abusing his enjoyment is much more tolerant for the long leaseholder than it is for the usufructuary. However, the burdens imposed on the long leaseholder are harder than those imposed on the usufructuary: he has to maintain the immovable and to do the normal repair works, even as he is responsible for all taxations (Article 9 Belgian Long Lease Act).[46] Besides, a right of long lease is also larger than a right of superficies: contrary to the maximum duration of fifty years of an independent right of superficies, the right of superficies that is linked to a right of long lease has a maximum duration that can vary between 27 and 99 years because of its accessory character. However, the owner is in a better position against the long leaseholder at the end: he can claim compensation and has no obligation to take over the buildings erected by the long leaseholder.[47]

Further, the long leaseholder has the right to change the purpose of the immovable property, on condition not to decrease its value (Article 3, first paragraph Belgian Long Lease Act). However, parties can – as frequently happens in practice – attribute in the long lease-agreement a certain purpose to the immovable. In that event, the long leaseholder can no longer change the purpose.[48] According to Dutch law, however, the right holder may change the purpose only with the consent of the owner (Article 5:89, paragraph 2 Dutch Civil Code). Conversely, parties cannot conventionally deviate from the requirement for the long leaseholder not to decrease the value of the immovable.[49] We can conclude that notwithstanding the comprehensive legally attributed rights of use and enjoyment, clauses are often inserted into the long-lease agreement in order to restrain the full right of enjoyment of the long leaseholder. For instance: the long leaseholder can also be forbidden to introduce whatever transformation to the immovable subject to the right of long lease.[50] Article 17 Belgian Long Lease Act recognizes the validity of such contractual arrangements, but restrictions to the right of enjoyment of the long leaseholder must be interpreted restrictively due to their deviation from the common law.[51]

3.1.5. Termination of the right of long lease

In principle, the right of long lease will end through the expiration of the term the parties agreed upon.[52] Moreover, the majority of the doctrine accepts that in the event of default by the long leaseholder or of the long lease-giver, one can appeal to the tacit dissolving

46 According to French law, the long leaseholder even is responsible for the great reparations (Terré & Simler 2010, p. 821, nr. 934; *bail à construction*: Article L251–4, second paragraph *Code de la construction et de l'habitation*).

47 Derine, Van Neste & Vandenberghe 1984, p. 857–858, nr. 1001D.

48 Dehan 1976, p. 506, nr. 41; Sagaert 2014, p. 571, nr. 709; Snaet 2008, p. 57, nr. 16; Van Oevelen 1992, p. 349, nr. 22.

49 Sagaert 2014, p. 571, nr. 709.

50 Dehan 1976, p. 506, nr. 41; Snaet 2008, p. 57, nr. 16.

51 Snaet 2008, p. 58, nr. 16; Van Oevelen 1990, p. 32, nr. 22; Van Oevelen 1992, p. 350, nr. 22.

52 *Belgium*: Claeys 2007, p. 44; Deli 1998, p. 69, nr. 100; Donnay 1974, p. 232, nr. 25; Hansenne 1996, p. 1242, nr. 1237; Mostin 2004, p. 118, nr. 97; Van Oevelen 1992, p. 339, nr. 13. *France*: Terré & Simler 2010, p. 822, nr. 935. *The Netherlands*: Article 3:81, second paragraph, b Dutch Civil Code.

condition (Article 1184 Belgian Civil Code) in order to end the right of long lease.[53] An explicit dissolving condition, with the consequence that in case of a default of the other party the agreement can be terminated without judicial authorization and on the basis of a mere unilateral expression of will, is also thought possible according to the majority of the doctrine and the jurisprudence.[54] Whereas the dissolution is in principle retroactive, an exception is made for duration agreements with successive or continual performances. The dissolution of such a reciprocal duration agreement of long lease takes effect only for the future, with the consequence that the performances that already were done as an execution of the agreement cannot and do not have to be given back.[55]

Besides, a right of long lease, like a right of usufruct but unlike a right of superficies, can also end due to the considerable damage the long leaseholder administered to the immovable or due to the abuse of his enjoyment (Article 15 Belgian Long Lease Act). The owner is then entitled to compensation. However, the long leaseholder, contrary to the usufructuary, has the right to avert the expiration of his right by repairing the immovable as it was before and by providing security for the future (Article 16 Belgian Long Lease Act). It is however uncertain if the expiration of the right of long lease can also be pronounced in the event of non-payment of the ground rent by the long leaseholder.[56]

The termination of the right of long lease also brings along the termination of the accessory right of superficies. Accession will occur and, consequently, the buildings, constructions and plantings will become property of the owner of the immovable without an obligation for the latter to pay compensation for it (Article 8 Belgian Long Lease Act).[57] It is, however, common to insert a clause concerning the destiny of the buildings, namely the right or the obligation for the long leaseholder to demolish them.[58] Parties can also agree for instance on the payment by the owner of the value of the buildings at the moment of the establishment of the right of long lease, the rest value at the end, the construction cost etc. Also the timing of the payment can be amended: in principle the compensation is due at the end of the right of long lease, but parties can also

53 *Belgium*: Lambert 1988, p. 314–323; Laurent 1887, p. 478, nr. 397; Sagaert 2014, p. 583–584, nr. 730; Snaet 2008, p. 52–53, nr. 10; Sterckx 1986, p. 544; Van Oevelen 1992, p. 340, nr. 13; Verbeke & Vanhove 2003, p. 88. *Contra* De Page 1953, p. 603, nr. 707, 2°, b; Derine, Van Neste & Vandenberghe 1984, p. 887, nr. 1017. *The Netherlands*: In the same sense: Article 5:87, first and third paragraph Dutch Civil Code.

54 Bergen 4 May 1998, *JLMB*, 1999, p. 444 and *Rec.gén.enr.not.*, 2000, p. 146; Bergen 17 May 1999, *Rec.gén.enr.not.*, 2000, p. 152; Rb. Ghent 13 December 1882, *Pas.*, 1883, III, p. 211; Rb. Brussels 13 February 1889, *Pas.*, 1889, III, p. 228; Laurent 1887, p. 479, nr. 397; Mostin 2004, p. 121, nr. 102; Snaet 2008, p. 53–54, nr. 11; Van Oevelen 1992, p. 351, nr. 23.

55 Cass. 24 January 1980, *Arr.Cass.*, 1979–80, p. 592, *Pas.*, 1980, I, p. 581 and *RW*, 1980–81, p. 1196; Cass. 31 January 1991, *Arr.Cass.*, 1990–91, p. 584, *Pas.*, 1991, I, p. 520 and *RW*, 1991–92, p. 774.

56 *Belgium*: Sagaert 2014, p. 581, nr. 727. *The Netherlands*: Termination of the right of long lease is possible when the long leaseholder is in default with the payment of the ground rent of two successive years (Article 5:87, second paragraph Dutch Civil Code).

57 *France*: The same applies to a *bail à construction* in the absence of a contractual regulation on that point: Article L251-2 *Code de la construction et de l'habitation*. *The Netherlands*: The long leaseholder is entitled to compensation (Article 5:99, first paragraph Dutch Civil Code).

58 Sagaert 2014, p. 586, nr. 733.

agree that it only has to be paid a certain period afterwards or even already at the moment of the completion of the building.[59]

3.2. *Right of usufruct*

3.2.1. Definition and application cases

Another property right that can be established on a church is a right of usufruct. The usufructuary has the temporary enjoyment of the church just like its owner, but subject to the obligation of preservation of the church (Article 578 Belgian and French Civil Code). A right of usufruct could be granted, for instance, to a legal person in order for him to use the church, during the term of the right of usufruct, for exhibitions, the establishment of a restaurant, the production of a play, rehearsals, or meetings of local associations etc. As the right of usufruct is established on an immovable, the deed through which the usufruct is established has to be registered at the mortgage registry office in order to have effect against third parties in good faith with a competing right (Article 1 Belgian Hypothec Act of 16 December 1851).[60]

3.2.2. Duration

Like a right of long lease, the duration of the right of usufruct is limited:[61] the maximum duration is linked with the length of the holder's life (Article 617, first paragraph Belgian and French Civil Code and Article 3:203, paragraph 2 Dutch Civil Code) or is 30 years when it's a legal person-usufructuary (Article 619 Belgian and French Civil Code and Article 3:203, paragraph 3 Dutch Civil Code).

3.2.3. Remuneration

Unlike a right of long lease, the establishment of a right of usufruct can, but does not have to be for valuable consideration.[62] However, when a right of usufruct is established on a church, it is obvious that there will be remuneration.

3.2.4. Rights and obligations of the usufructuary

During the right of usufruct, the usufructuary has the competence to use the immovable on two conditions. Consequently, the competence of the usufructuary to use is more

59 Sagaert 2014, p. 587, nr. 734.

60 Claeys 2007, p. 67; Carette & Del Corral 2012, p. 2–3, nr. 2; Snaet 2008, p. 73, nr. 45; Vits 1998, p. 11–12, nr. 4.

61 That is a rule of public order, contractual divergences are thus absolutely void (Claeys 2007, p. 18; Dekkers & Dirix 2005, p. 183, nr. 457; De Page 1953, p. 157, nr. 195; Derine, Van Neste & Vandenberghe 1984, p. 341, nr. 843; Kluyskens 1953, p. 224, nr. 214; Laurent 1887, p. 413, nr. 325 and p. 445, nr. 352).

62 Hansenne 1996, p. 1239, nr. 1232; Snaet 2008, p. 73, nr. 44; Vits 1998, p. 16, nr. 18.

restricted than the competence of a long leaseholder. On the one hand, the usufructuary cannot change the purpose of the church without the consent of the bare owner.[63] He is indeed obliged to maintain the good on which the right of usufruct is established (Article 587 Belgian and French Civil Code). This restriction on the competence of the usufructuary is advantageous for the bare owner of a church: even without an additional stipulation, he can be sure of the maintenance of the original purpose of the building during the right of usufruct: changing the purpose without his consent can lead to the expiration of the right of usufruct (Article 618 Belgian and French Civil Code). However, nothing prevents the parties to deviate contractually from the aforementioned obligation,[64] although the right of usufruct then immediately poaches on the territory of a right of long lease.[65] On the other hand, the usufructuary has to exercise his right of use as a *bonus pater familias*,[66] under penalty of expiration of his right in case of abuse in Belgium and France (Article 618 Belgian and French Civil Code), and in the Netherlands under penalty of attribution of the management to the bare owner or administering the right of usufruct (Article 3:221, paragraph 1 Dutch Civil Code). It's for that purpose that the bare owner has a general right of control and supervision on the management by the usufructuary.[67] However, this obligation for the usufructuary to manage the good subject to a right of usufruct as a *bonus pater familias* can also be contractually adapted and the liability of the usufructuary can be increased as well as lightened.[68] Through such adaptations, the right of enjoyment of the usufructuary does not differ greatly from that of the holder of a right of superficies.[69]

Furthermore, the usufructuary, like the long leaseholder and with respect for the purpose of the good subject to the right of usufruct, also enjoys an accessory right of superficies, so he has the right to build or rebuild.[70] Moreover, during the right of usufruct he will be owner of the buildings, constructions and plants he set up.[71] Although Article 599, second paragraph Belgian and French Civil Code indicates that the usufructuary will under no circumstances claim remuneration for the improvements he has installed, even if the value of the immovable would have been increased

63 *Belgium*: Cass. 27 September 1957, *Pas.*, 1958, I, p. 58; De Page 1953, p. 265, nr. 333B; Derine, Van Neste & Vandenberghe 1984, p. 440, nr. 873; Hansenne 1996, p. 1038, nr. 1019; Snaet 2008, p. 84, nr. 74. *France*: Malaurie 2003, p. 254, nr. 828. *The Netherlands*: Article 3:208, first paragraph Dutch Civil Code.

64 Dekkers & Dirix 2005, p. 215, nr. 541; Jansen & Swinnen 2012, p. 84, nr. 55; Vits 1998, p. 20, nr. 35. However, that reneging can also be balanced. For instance, one can stipulate in the agreement that the usufructuary can change the purpose on condition that the bare owner previously agrees by letter, or one or more particular purposes can be fixed into which the usufructuary can change the current purpose of the good subject to the right of usufruct (Jansen & Swinnen 2012, p. 84, nr. 55).

65 Sagaert 2014, p. 407, nr. 501.

66 Hansenne 1996, p. 1054, nr. 1041; Snaet 2008, p. 87, nr. 77; Vits 1998, p. 20, nr. 33.

67 Verbeke 1999, p. 557, nrs. 84–85.

68 Carette & Del Corral 2012, p. 10, nr. 10.

69 Carette & Del Corral 2012, p. 11, nr. 10.

70 Jansen & Swinnen 2012, p. 53, nr. 6; Sagaert 2014, p. 408, nr. 502.

71 Sagaert 2014, p. 408, nr. 502; Snaet 2008, p. 59, nr. 19.

accordingly, that starting point has to be qualified: renovations or construction works that exceed the normal management of the usufructuary will qualify for remuneration on the basis of unjust enrichment.[72] Moreover, the usufructuary can exercise his lien (retention of title) on those buildings as long as the bare owner – who becomes owner of the constructions set up by the usufructuary at the end of the right of usufruct – has not fulfilled his remuneration-obligation.[73] Further, the usufructuary also has the right to perform acts of preservation or management (the usufructuary can even lease out the church[74] or give it on loan (Article 595 Belgian and French Civil Code and Article 3:217, paragraph 1 Dutch Civil Code)),[75] and he can even allow a right of usufruct, a right of superficies or a servitude within the boundaries of his own right.[76]

When the personality of the usufructuary is important for the bare owner, one can insert into the agreement a prohibition to alienate with the consequence that the right of usufruct becomes *intuitu personae* and so can only be exercised by the current usufructuary.[77] Also, a less far-reaching restriction is possible, for instance a right of preference.

Finally, the usufructuary accounts for the normal charges (Article 608 Belgian and French Civil Code, Article 3:220, paragraph 1 Dutch Civil Code) such as taxations[78], unless parties agree otherwise[79], even as he is responsible for the maintenance reparations of the building (Articles 605–606 Belgian and French Civil Code, Article 3:220, paragraph 1 Dutch Civil Code), such as the paintwork, the plastwork and reparations of floors, ceilings and the roof.[80] During the right of usufruct, the usufructuary can be obliged to do those maintenance reparations and its non-fulfilment can even cause the

72 So, the lowest of the two amounts (the surplus value the building has given to the ground and the cost of the building) will be refunded. Sagaert 2014, p. 408, nr. 502. In the same sense: Jansen & Swinnen 2012, p. 54, nr. 6; Snaet 2008, p. 98, nrs. 98–99. Or, according to the classic authors: on the basis of Article 555 Belgian Civil Code (Dekkers & Dirix 2005, p. 246, nr. 620; De Page 1953, p. 379, nr. 467C; Derine, Van Neste & Vandenberghe 1984, p. 549–550, nr. 908; Hansenne 1996, p. 1042, nr. 1019).

73 Sagaert 2014, p. 408, nr. 502.

74 In that case, the lease will not end with the decease of the usufructuary, but the owner will always have to respect a lease (with fixed date (Article 1328 Belgian Civil Code)) with a duration of maximum nine years (Dekkers & Dirix 2005, p. 208, nr. 522; Hansenne 1996, p. 1033, nr. 1016; Sagaert 2014, p. 409, nr. 503; Vits 1998, p. 22, nr. 38).

75 Although the agreement also can determine that the usufructuary can not establish personal rights on the good subject to the right of usufruct (Jansen & Swinnen 2012, p. 73, nr. 38).

76 Jansen & Swinnen 2012, p. 55, nr. 7; Sagaert 2014, p. 414, nr. 508.

77 Jansen & Swinnen 2012, p. 72, nr. 36.

78 *Belgium*: For instance the direct taxes with regard to the good subject to the right of usufruct, the immovable advance tax payment, vacancy levy etc. (Sagaert 2014, p. 422, nr. 519). *France*: the normal taxations (Malaurie 2003, p. 256, nr. 829).

79 Either advantageous for the bare owner or for the usufructuary (Sagaert 2014, p. 422, nr. 519; Snaet 2008, p. 91, nr. 85; Vits 1998, p. 29, nr. 63).

80 Sagaert 2014, p. 419, nr. 516.

expiration of his right.[81] This obligation can in that way be helpful to an owner who is in difficulties with the maintenance costs of the building. However, the bare owner is still liable for the great reparations[82] (Article 605, second paragraph Belgian and French Civil Code). Also the bare owner can, according to Belgian law but not French law, during the right of usufruct, be obliged to fulfil his obligation to account for the great reparations.[83]

3.2.5. Termination of the right of usufruct

The right of usufruct will end with the decease of the holder of the right of usufruct (even when the stipulated term has not yet expired)[84], with the expiration of the stipulated term,[85] or with the dissolution of the legal person (even when the thirty-year-term has not yet expired)[86] (Article 617 Belgian and French Civil Code). Also, contractual termination reasons can be agreed upon, such as cancellation stipulations and resolutive conditions. Moreover, when the right of usufruct was established for valuable consideration, Article 1184 Belgian Civil Code will apply when the usufructuary does not fulfil his obligations.[87] Finally, the right of usufruct can also be terminated when the usufructuary abuses his enjoyment, through damaging the property or letting the property fall into decay for lack of maintenance (Article 618 Belgian and French Civil Code). The bare owner could, for instance, invoke the expiration of the right of usufruct when the usufructuary does not observe the purpose of the good subject to the right of usufruct.[88] Termination of the right of usufruct presents for the usufructuary the

81 Derine, Van Neste & Vandenberghe 1984, p. 476–477, nr. 886; Hansenne 1996, p. 1061, nr. 1047; Sagaert 2014, p. 419, nr. 516; Snaet 2008, p. 89, nr. 82.

82 Large renovation and conversion works with a view to the general solidity and the maintenance of the whole building and which are really an exception in the existence of the property and from which the costs normally are withdrawn from the capital (Cass. 22 January 1970, *Arr.Cass.*, 1970, p. 465, *RW*, 1969–70, p. 1535 and *RCJB*, 1971, p. 463, note Hansenne; Liège 7 July 1998, *TBBR*, 2001, p. 107). However, the mere fact that the constructions have an important financial repercussion will not be sufficient to decide to the classification of great reparation (Sagaert 2014, p. 420, nr. 517). *The Netherlands*: In case of great reparations, the usufructuary is obliged to give notice of that necessity to the bare owner and to give him the opportunity to repair; however, the latter is not obliged to do that (Article 3:220, paragraph 1 Dutch Civil Code).

83 *Belgium*: De Page 1953, p. 277, nr. 342; Derine, Van Neste & Vandenberghe 1984, p. 480–485, nr. 888; Laurent 1887, p. 685, nr. 548; Sagaert 2014, p. 421, nr. 518. *Contra* Kluyskens 1953, p. 214, nr. 202. *France*: Cass. 10 December 1900, *S.*, 1904, 1, 36; Cass. 30 January 1970, *Bull. Civ*, III, nr. 83; Cass. 10 July 2002, *Rev. Loyers*, 2002, p. 562, note Remy; Atias 2014, p. 177, nr. 234; Malaurie 2003, p. 257, nr. 832; Terré & Simler 2010, p. 733, nr. 825. *Contra* Zénati-Castaing & Revet 2008, p. 497, nr. 338.

84 *Belgium*: Claeys 2007, p. 22; Dekkers & Dirix 2005, p. 189, nr. 471; Hansenne 1996, p. 1022, nr. 999 and p. 1077, nr. 1068; Snaet 2008, p. 75, nr. 51; Vits 1998, p. 13. *France*: Atias 2014, p. 183, nr. 246; Bergel, Bruschi & Cimamonti 2009, 312, nr. 271; Terré & Simler 2010, p. 697, nr. 778.

85 Claeys 2007, p. 287; Derine, Van Neste & Vandenberghe 1984, p. 523; Snaet 2008, p. 93, nr. 89; Vits 1998, p. 30, nr. 70.

86 Derine, Van Neste & Vandenberghe 1984, p. 524, nr. 897; Hansenne 1996, p. 1077, nr. 1068; Snaet 2008, p. 75, nr. 52.

87 Sagaert 2014, p. 438, nr. 541.

88 Claeys 2007, p. 293; Dekkers & Dirix 2005, p. 238, nr. 602; De Page 1953, p. 268, nr. 335B; Kluyskens 1953, p. 177, nr. 155; Hansenne 1996, p. 1082, nr. 1075.

obligation to return the concerned good.[89] However, depreciations due to the normal use of the good subject to the right of usufruct will not incur the liability of the usufructuary (Article 589 Belgian and French Civil Code).

3.3. *Right of superficies*

3.3.1. Definition and application cases

Finally, parties can also agree to establish a right of superficies on the church, through which a temporary horizontal division of the ownership of the land on the one hand, and of the constructed buildings, constructions or plants, on the other hand, arises.[90] As a consequence, the right of use of the right holder is much more restricted and merely oriented at the construction.[91] The right of superficies can refer to already set up buildings, constructions or plants as well as to those which still have to be set up.[92] However, parties can conventionally determine the extensiveness of the right, for instance by allowing the holder of the right of superficies only to set up a well-defined construction.[93] The holder of the right of superficies however does not have a property right on the ground.[94] When the right of superficies is established through an agreement, there is no formal requirement in the mutual relation between the holder of the right of superficies and the landowner, but a deed is required and has to be registered at the mortgage registry office with a view for the right of superficies to have effect against third parties in good faith with a competing right (Article 3 Belgian Superficies Act[95]).[96]

Whereas the Belgian Superficies Act gave rise to doubts concerning the question whether a right of superficies could be used for the installation of solar panels on the roof of a

89 *Belgium*: Dekkers & Dirix 2005, p. 243, nr. 614; De Page 1953, p. 366, nr. 453; Derine, Van Neste & Vandenberghe 1984, p. 544, nr. 907; Hansenne 1996, p. 1068, nr. 1058; Kluyskens 1953, p. 220, nr. 209; Snaet 2008, p. 84, nr. 75; Vits 1998, p. 33, nr. 84. *France*: Bergel, Bruschi & Cimamonti 2009, p. 309, nr. 266. *The Netherlands*: Article 3:225 Dutch Civil Code.

90 *Belgium*: Deli 1998, p. 39, nr. 7; Kluyskens 1953, p. 247, nr. 247; Puelinckx & Boven 2006, p. 323–324; Sagaert 2014, p. 591, nr. 738; Snaet 2008, p. 59, nr. 17; Vandenberghe & Viaene 2006, p. 35, nr. 3; Van Oevelen 1992, p. 353, nr. 24. *France*: Bergel, Bruschi & Cimamonti 2009, p. 327, nr. 285; Terré & Simler 2010, p. 817, nr. 927. *The Netherlands*: De Jong & Ploeger 2008, p. 73, nr. 47; Snijders & Rank-Berenschot 2012, p. 565, nr. 683.

91 Puelinckx & Boven 2006, p. 326; Verstappen 2004, p. 7, nr. 12.

92 De Page 1953, p. 579, nr. 684; Derine, Van Neste & Vandenberghe 1984, p. 915, nr. 1024; Mostin 2004, p. 142, nr. 137.

93 Snaet 2008, p. 60, nr. 21.

94 Carette & Del Corral 2012, p. 7, nr. 8; Claeys 2007, p. 40.

95 Act 10 January 1824 on the right of superficies, *BS*, 10 January 1824 as modified by Article 124 Act 25 April 2014 on diverse provisions concerning Justice, *BS*, 14 May 2014, p. 39.045.

96 Cass. 13 May 1970, *Pas.*, 1969, I, p. 801; Claeys 2007, p. 39; Deli 1998, p. 55, nr. 53; De Page 1953, p. 583, nr. 691, 1°; Hansenne 1996, p. 1250, nr. 1243; Kluyskens 1953, p. 249, nr. 248; Mostin 2004, p. 146, nr. 144; Sagaert 2014, p. 609, nr. 764; Vandenberghe & Viaene 2006, p. 44, nr. 36; Van Oevelen 1992, p. 355, nr. 25; Verstappen 2004, p. 8, nr. 17.

building because of the use of the words 'on another man's *land*', the 2014-amendment took away those doubts: a right of superficies can be used for constructions on or under the ground and a right of superficies can with certainty rest on another man's building.[97] Dutch law was already clear on that point.[98] Thus, it is possible to install solar panels on a roof which is not your property, on the basis of a right of superficies.[99] In such case, parties must accurately describe the object of the agreement: the right of superficies cannot be limited to the solar panels as such, but must also refer to all accessories, such as the connection to the grid, the cables, links and transformers.[100] It is even recommended that parties stipulate the acquisition of the required permits, connections, studies and subsidies as a suspensive condition in the superficies agreement,[101] with the consequence that the effect of the agreement depends on the fulfilment of those conditions. A right of superficies cannot only be used for the installation of solar panels, but also for the installation of aerials for mobile data traffic.[102]

3.3.2. Duration

Just like a right of long lease or a right of usufruct, a right of superficies is characterized by a restriction of time: the maximum duration of a right of superficies is fifty years under Belgian law (Article 4 Belgian Superficies Act), and this contrasts with the parties freedom on that point under Dutch law (Article 5:104, paragraph 2 *jo.* Article 5:86 Dutch Civil Code) and its presumed perpetual character under French law.[103] As the right of long lease, a right of superficies that is allowed for a period longer than fifty years will be reduced to the legal maximum duration.[104] That term can however be renewed (an indefinite number of times), explicitly or silently (Article 4 Belgian Superficies Act).[105] It is possible to skirt that restriction only through the effect of an accessory right of superficies, i.e. a right of superficies linked to, for instance, a (perpetual) servitude: the accessory right of superficies will last as long as the principal right.[106] However, this does

97 Bill 26 November 2013 on diverse provisions concerning Justice, *Parl.St.*, Chamber 2013–14, nr. 3149, p. 108.

98 Article 5:101, first paragraph Dutch Civil Code: *'Het recht van opstal is een zakelijk recht om in, op of boven een onroerende zaak van een ander gebouwen, werken of beplantingen in eigendom te hebben of te verkrijgen.'* (free translation: 'A right of superficies is a real property right which enables its proprietor to have or acquire for himself buildings, constructions or plants in, on or above *an immovable thing* owned by someone else.').

99 Sagaert & Bouly 2014, p. 1463, nr. 6.

100 Vandorpe & Haverbeke 2010, p. 6.

101 Vandorpe & Haverbeke 2010, p. 6.

102 *Belgium*: Timmermans 2011, p. 1126, nr. 677. *The Netherlands*: Snijders & Rank-Berenschot 2012, p. 567, nr. 685.

103 Bergel, Bruschi & Cimamonti 2009, p. 337, nr. 295; Malaurie 2003, p. 268, nr. 904; Terré & Simler 2010, p. 838, nr. 953.

104 Cass. 15 December 2006, *Pas.*, 2006, 2713, *TBO*, 2007, 68, *T.Not.*, 2008, 104 and *RW*, 2007–08, 104, note Muylle; Derine, Van Neste & Vandenberghe 1984, p. 907, nr. 1021; Kluyskens 1953, p. 248, nr. 247; Mostin 2004, p. 139, nr. 130; Snaet 2008, p. 63, nr. 25; Van Oevelen 1992, p. 355, nr. 25.

105 Dekkers & Dirix 2005, p. 288, nr. 727; De Page 1953, p. 580, nr. 685; Mostin 2004, p. 140, nr. 133.

106 Deli 1998, p. 1249, nr. 1240; Sagaert 2014, p. 596, nr. 747; Snaet 2008, p. 60, nr. 19.

not seem to be a problem for the installation of solar panels since they have an average life expectancy of twenty to twenty-five years. Moreover, in principle the landowner will be obliged to pay compensation at the termination of an independent right of superficies (Article 6 Belgian Superficies Act)[107] (unless conventionally modified)[108], which is not the case when it is an accessory right of superficies.[109] Unlike a right of long lease, no minimal duration applies here.

3.3.3. Remuneration

Unlike a right of long lease, a right of superficies does not have to be for valuable consideration.[110] When parties nevertheless agree upon a fee ('*solarium*') – for instance, through the delivery of electricity at a reduced price – it can just as well be a periodic fee[111] as a once-only fee.[112]

3.3.4. Rights and obligations of the holder of a right of superficies

It is essential for the holder of a right of superficies to have the competence to build on another man's land.[113] Conversely, a right of superficies cannot facilitate transformations, renovations, reparations, improvements or restorations of an existent building:[114] such works are incorporated immediately in the building, so that a horizontal division of ownership is impossible.[115] During the right of superficies, the constructions set up by the holder of the right of superficies remain his property.[116] However, the rights of use and enjoyment of the holder of a right of superficies are much more restricted than those of a long leaseholder: the former has no property right of use and enjoyment on the land

107 Moreover, the holder of a right of superficies can exercise a lien (right of retention) on the constructions as long als the landowner has not paid the compensation (Mostin 2004, p. 155, nr. 164; Sagaert 2014, p. 618, nr. 782).

108 Verstappen 2004, p. 25, nr. 52.

109 Sagaert 2014, p. 597–598, nr. 747.

110 *Belgium*: Deli 1998, p. 49, nr. 38; de Montpellier 2003, p. 25, nr. 48; Derine, Van Neste & Vandenberghe 1984, p. 288, nr. 728 and p. 916, nr. 1025; Hansenne 1996, p. 1255, nr. 1252; Mostin 2004, p. 158, nr. 172; Puelinckx & Boven 2006, p. 325; Snaet 2008, p. 64, nr. 27; Vandenberghe & Viaene 2006, p. 39, nr. 15; Van Oevelen 1992, p. 360, nr. 30; Verstappen 2004, p. 22, nr. 44. *The Netherlands*: Article 5:101, third paragraph Dutch Civil Code.

111 The amount of the fee can even periodically fluctuate (Verstappen 2004, p. 22, nr. 45). Vandorpe & Haverbeke 2010, p. 5.

112 De Montpellier 2003, p. 25, nr. 48; Mostin 2004, p. 158, nr. 172; Sagaert 2014, p. 620, nr. 785; Vandorpe & Haverbeke 2010, p. 5.

113 Hansenne 1996, p. 1251, nr. 1246; Sagaert 2014, p. 592, nr. 738.

114 Rb. Kortrijk 14 November 1947, *T.Not.*, 1950, 17; Derine, Van Neste & Vandenberghe 1984, p. 915, nr. 1024.

115 Rb. Brussels 26 October 2001, *T.Not.*, 2003, 488; Snaet 2008, p. 61, nr. 21.

116 *Belgium*: Derine, Van Neste & Vandenberghe 1984, p. 906, nr. 1021; Sagaert 2014, p. 606, nr. 761. *France*: Bergel, Bruschi & Cimamonti 2009, p. 338, nr. 297.

nor on the buildings already staying on the land that were not included in the agreement, he only has the right to set up.

3.3.5. Termination of the right of superficies

Article 9 Belgian Superficies Act determines in a non-exhaustive way the reasons for termination of a right of superficies, namely confusion, loss of the land and the extinctive thirty-years prescription. Besides, the right of superficies will also come to an end through expiration of the stipulated term.[117] Parties can also agree upon additional reasons of termination, such as cancellations,[118] explicit or tacit (Article 1184 Belgian Civil Code) dissolving conditions,[119] and resolutive conditions.[120] At the end of the right, the landowner becomes owner of the constructions, but only on payment of their value (Article 6 Belgian Superficies Act).

4. Adaptation of the contract of sale of a church

Clause of purpose restriction

When the owner of the church nevertheless decides to sell the church, parties can opt for the insertion in the agreement of a clause of purpose restriction. That clause guarantees protection of the sacred character of the building. Through such a perpetual clause (*kettingbeding*) the original owner (A) stipulates that the purchaser (B) enters into the obligation not to change the purpose of the building towards the original owner (and for instance, not to use it as a party-location). Further, B also has to force the next purchaser (C) not to change the purpose of the building towards the original owner (as a stipulation on behalf of a third party (*derdenbeding*)) and to insert the clause in a subsequent sale agreement.[121]

However, this clause does not offer its beneficiary adequate protection. If the clause is breached by virtue of the clause not be inserted in a subsequent transfer, the beneficiary will be entitled to compensation. But that sanction offers no protection in the event of the insolvency of the successor responsible for the breach, while the beneficiary is not in a contractual relationship with that person and thus, could not evaluate his solvency.[122] Exceptionally, the beneficiary of the perpetual clause will be able to address the

117 Claeys 2007, p. 40; Dekkers & Dirix 2005, p. 289, nr. 730; Derine, Van Neste & H. Vandenberghe 1984, p. 927, nr. 1032; Hansenne 1996, p. 1258, nr. 1256; Mostin 2004, p. 162, nr. 185; Van Oevelen 1992, p. 364, nr. 34.

118 Muylle 2012, p. 335, nr. 472; Sagaert 2014, p. 616, nr. 778; Snaet 2008, p. 64, nr. 26.

119 Mostin 2004, p. 164, nr. 190; Sagaert 2014, p. 617, nr. 779.

120 Sagaert 2014, p. 617, nr. 779; Snaet 2008, p. 64, nr. 26.

121 Sagaert 2005, p. 356, nr. 16.

122 Sagaert 2005, p. 357, nr. 18.

purchaser by virtue of his participation as a third party in the breach of a contractual duty.[123]

Through his explicit or tacit consent to the perpetual clause the purchaser is obliged to respect the restriction on purpose. The third party, C, however, is in no way obliged to agree with that obligation. If the chain is broken through the making of an agreement without the obligation for C to comply with the obligation, B commits a contractual default towards A, with contractual liability as a consequence.[124] Moreover, when the stipulation is also a stipulation on behalf of third party, the original beneficiary can directly address the successor who broke the chain.[125] But in the absence of a stipulation on behalf of a third party, the original beneficiary can only address himself to the successor responsible for the breach if the latter was or, had to be, aware of the clause and so participated as a third party in the breach of a contractual duty.[126] However, the effectiveness of the clause can be increased by linking the breach of it to a penal clause or to other sanctions.[127]

The question arises whether the perpetual clause has to be respected in the event of an enforced sale, that means within the framework of an enforcement (e.g. seizure, bankruptcy). After all, creditors may not experience negative consequences of an occult stipulation that weighs on the value of the goods. Consequently, when the register of mortgages does not prove the perpetual clause, the creditor is given priority over the beneficiary of the perpetual clause. In contrast, when the register of mortgages does prove the perpetual clause, for instance, because it is part of the transfer agreement that was integrally registered, then the principle of anteriority applies: the perpetual clause can be enforced against mortgagees or seizers who registered later, but not to creditors who precedingly and in good faith had acquired a property right and who registered that at the mortgage registry office.[128] It is thus recommended that the clause of purpose restriction is also proved at the mortgage registry office.

5. Conclusion

When the owner of a church decides to sell the building or to establish a property right on it, then the first question is whether the concerned church is a public land good or not. If it is, then there has to be a decision of change of use, or one has to evaluate in the concrete if the establishment of a property right is compatible with the purpose of the church for everyone's use. When that is done, property law still offers a lot of possibilities. Depending on the desires of the concerned parties, one can opt for a right of long lease, a right of usufruct or a right of superficies. However, one

123 Verhoeven 1988–89, p. 164–165.
124 Carette 2011, p. 40, nr. 49; Sagaert 2005, p. 358, nr. 19.
125 Sagaert 2005, p. 358, nr. 19.
126 Carette 2011, p. 40, nr. 49.
127 Sagaert 2011, p. 156.
128 Sagaert 2005, p. 359, nr. 19.

should not lose sight of the fact that each of those rights can be adapted on a lot of points. When the owner of the church decides to sell the church, a clause of purpose restriction can meet the owner's wishes to conserve the sacred character of the building.

With these property law-related answers to the problems caused by the decline in church attendance, we can hope that those buildings can get another useful purpose so that we do not have to lose those often wonderful landmarks.

Bibliography

Books

Atias 2014
Atias, C., *Droit civil: les biens*, Paris: LexisNexis, 2014.

Bergel, Bruschi & Cimamonti 2009
Bergel, J.-L., Bruschi, M. & Cimamonti, S., *Les biens*, Paris: LGDJ, 2009.

Claeys 2007
Claeys, D., *Usufruit et nue-propriété: principes et actualités*, Waterloo: Kluwer, 2007.

De Jong & Ploeger 2008
De Jong, J. & Ploeger, H. D., *Erfpacht en opstal*, Deventer: Kluwer, 2008.

Dekkers & Dirix 2005
Dekkers, R. & Dirix, E., *Handboek Burgerlijk Recht*, II, *Zakenrecht, zekerheden, verjaring*, Antwerp: Intersentia, 2005.

De Page 1953
De Page, H., *Traité élémentaire de droit civil belge: principes, doctrine, jurisprudence*, VI, *Les biens. Les sûretés*, Brussels: Bruylant, 1953.

Derine, Van Neste & Vandenberghe 1984
Derine, R., Van Neste, F. & Vandenberghe, H., *Zakenrecht* in *Beginselen van Belgisch privaatrecht*, IIB, Ghent: Story-Scientia, 1984.

Hansenne 1996
Hansenne, J., *Les biens: précis*, II, Liège: Université de Liège. Faculté de droit, 1996.

Kluyskens 1953
Kluyskens, A., *Zakenrecht* in *Beginselen van burgerlijk recht*, V, Antwerp: Standaard, 1953.

Laurent 1887
Laurent, F., *Principes de droit civil*, VIII, Brussels: Bruylant-Christophe, 1887.

Malaurie 2003
Malaurie, P., *Les biens*, Paris: Defrénois, 2003.

Muylle 2012
Muylle, M., *De duur en de beëindiging van zakelijke rechten*, Antwerp: Intersentia, 2012.

Sagaert 2014
Sagaert, V., *Goederenrecht* in *Beginselen van Belgisch privaatrecht*, 5, Mechelen: Kluwer, 2014.

Snijders & Rank-Berenschot 2012
Snijders, H.J. & Rank-Berenschot, E.B., *Goederenrecht*, Deventer: Kluwer, 2012.

Terré & Simler 2010
Terré, F. & Simler, P., *Droit civil: les biens*, Paris: Dalloz, 2010.

Timmermans 2011
Timmermans, R., *Zakenrechtelijke modellen voor uitgifte van bouwprojecten: gedwongen mede-eigendom, appartementsmede-eigendom, erfpacht, opstal, verdiepingseigendom en volume-eigendom* in *Reeks notariële praktijkstudies*, Mechelen: Kluwer, 2011.

Verstappen 2004
Verstappen, J., *Erfpacht, opstal en vruchtgebruik*, Brussels: Larcier, 2004.

Waline 1936
Waline, M., *Manuel élémentaire de droit administratif*, Paris: Sirey, 1936.

Zénati-Castaing & Revet 2008
Zénati-Castaing, F. & Revet, T., *Les biens*, Paris: PUF, 2008.

Articles in compilations

Carette & Del Corral 2012
Carette, N. & Del Corral, J., 'De kwalificatie van het recht van vruchtgebruik: contractuele mogelijkheden en afbakening tegenover opstal, erfpacht en huur', in: Sagaert, V. & Verbeke, A.-L. (ed.), *Vruchtgebruik: mogelijkheden, beperkingen en innovaties*, Antwerp: Intersentia, 2012, p. 1–50.

Dehan 1976
Dehan, P., 'L'utilisation actuelle de l'emphytéose, de la superficie, du bail et du mandat à des fins autres que celles prévues par le législateur', in: Flamme, M.-A., Hannequart, Y. & Hoeffler, J., *Le droit de la construction et de l'urbanisme*, Brussels: Jeune barreau, 1976, p. 475–548.

Deli 1998
Deli, D., 'Erfpacht en opstal: burgerrechtelijke aspecten', in: Meulemans, D. (ed.), *Vruchtgebruik, erfpacht en opstal*, Antwerp: Maklu, 1998, p. 37–74.

de Montpellier 2003
de Montpellier, F., 'Usufruit, emphytéose et superficie. Limites de l'autonomie de la volonté et utilisation combinée', in: Dierckx, F. (ed.), *Onroerend goed als beleggingsinstrument*, Brussels: De Boeck en Larcier, 2003, p. 1–46.

Jansen & Swinnen 2012
Jansen, R. & Swinnen, K., 'De contractuele modulering van de gebruiks- en beschikkingsbevoegdheden van de vruchtgebruiker', in: Sagaert, V. & Verbeke, A.-L. (ed.), *Vruchtgebruik: mogelijkheden, beperkingen en innovaties*, Antwerp: Intersentia, 2012, p. 51–90.

Lecocq 2000
Lecocq, P., 'Superficie et emphytéose: questions d'actualité', in: Lecocq, P. & Pâcques, M. (ed.), *Le point sur le droit des biens*, I, *Les aspects de droit privé*, Liège: Ulg. Formation permanente CUP, 2000, p. 129–156.

Mostin 2004
Mostin, C., 'Emphytéose et superficie - Aspects civils', in: *Répertoire notarial*, II, *Les biens*, 6, Brussels: Larcier, 2004, p. 65–164.

Puelinckx &Boven 2006
Puelinckx, P. & Boven, L., 'Erfpacht en opstal: een actuele erfenis', in: Barbaix, R. & Swennen, F. (ed.), *Over erven: liber amicorum Mieken Puelinckx-Coene*, Mechelen: Kluwer, 2006, p. 317–350.

Snaet 2008
Snaet, S., 'Alternatieve vormen voor het verwerven van onroerend goed: erfpacht, opstal en vruchtgebruik', in: Verhoeye, J., De Coninck, H., Snaet, S., Janssen, D., Beyaert, S., Timmermans, R., Flamey, P., Bosquet, J., Ceenaeme, J., Roelandts, B., Van Landeghem, H. & De Smedt, P., *Het onroerend goed in de verschillende takken van het recht*, Ghent: Larcier, 2008, p. 47–99.

Van Oevelen 1990
Van Oevelen, A., 'Overeenkomsten op basis van het recht van erfpacht en het recht van opstal. Onroerende leasing: een theoretisch kader', in: Van Oevelen, A., Van Poucke, P. & Van de Velde, J. (ed.), *Oude en nieuwe rechtsfiguren: erfpacht, opstal, onroerende leasing, time-sharing*, Antwerp: Kluwer rechtswetenschappen, 1990, p. 7–67.

Van Oevelen 1992
Van Oevelen, A., 'Actuele ontwikkelingen inzake het recht van erfpacht en het recht van opstal', in: Casman, H., De Corte, R. & Dirix, E., *Het zakenrecht, absoluut niet een rustig bezit*, Antwerp: Kluwer rechtswetenschappen, 1992, p. 321–374.

Vits 1998
Vits, P., 'Vruchtgebruik: burgerrechtelijke aspecten', in: Meulemans, D. (ed.), *Vruchtgebruik, erfpacht en opstal*, Antwerp: Maklu, 1998, p. 11–36.

Articles in journals

Carton de Tournai & Charlier 1971
Carton de Tournai, R. & Charlier, A.J., 'Quelques considérations d'actualité sur l'emphytéose et la superficie', *JT*, 1971, p. 69–72.

Donnay 1974
Donnay, M., 'L'emphytéose', *Rec.gén.enr.not.*, 1974, p. 209–242.

Lambert 1988
Lambert, M., 'Emphytéose et condition résolutoire tacite', *Rev.not.b.*, 1988, p. 314–323.

Ravanas 2009
Ravanas, E., 'Quelques réflexions autour de problématiques immobilières rencontrées dans les projets éoliens et photovoltaïques', *JCP N*, 2009, nr. 40, p. 15–21.

Sagaert & Bouly 2014
Sagaert, V. & Bouly, S., 'Een te restrictieve omschrijving voor het voorwerp van een opstalrecht?' (note under Cass. 13 September 2013), *RW*, 2013–14, p. 1461–1464.

Sterckx 1986
Sterckx, D., 'L'emphytéose et la condition résolutoire tacite' (note under Brussels 19 February 1986), *Rev.not.b.*, 1986, p. 542–544.

Vandenberghe & Viaene 2006
Vandenberghe, H. & Viaene, T., 'Actuele ontwikkelingen inzake erfpacht en opstal', *TBO*, 2006, p. 34–55.

Vandorpe & Haverbeke 2010
Vandorpe, W. & Haverbeke, D., 'De praktijk van opstalovereenkomsten voor zonnepanelenprojecten', *Nieuwsbrief Notariaat*, 2010, afl. 2, p. 4–7.

Verbeke 1999
Verbeke, A., 'Creatief met vruchtgebruik', *T.Not.*, 1999, p. 530–579.

Verhoeven 1988–89
Verhoeven, A., 'De juridische grondslag van kwalitatieve rechten en plichten', *Jura Falc.*, 1988–89, p. 143–168.

Werdefroy 1983
Werdefroy, F., 'Beschouwingen over de onroerende natrekking, het recht van erfpacht, het recht van opstal en het verlof tot bouwen', *TPR*, 1983, p. 293–342.

Laurens de Hoog

THE FIRST IN TIME RULE IN HISTORICAL CONTEXT

1. Introduction

Creditors run the risk of not being repaid in full, especially in the event of insolvency of the debtor. Theoretically all creditors can recover their debt from the proceeds of liquidation. In legal systems based on Roman law, every creditor is satisfied in accordance with the principle of *paritas creditorum* (equality of creditors) on a pro rata-basis, which means that the proceeds will be divided in proportion to how much each is owed. In practice however, these creditors receive, on average, no payment at all.

The above does not apply to secured creditors, who have taken proprietary security from debtors to support the repayment of loans or other obligations. Traditionally this can take the form of the fiduciary transfer of property (*fiducia cum creditore*), possessory security (*pignus*) or consensual security (*hypotheca*).[1] In the event of the debtor's insolvency, secured creditors take priority over unsecured creditors.[2]

Contrary to *fiducia* and *pignus,* non-possessory security interests can be given over the same asset more than once. When this is the case and all secured creditors enforce their hypothec while the claims exceed the value of the charged property, it is relevant to determine the order of priority between those security interests. The basic principle of priority between security interests can be reduced to four words by Roman Emperor Caracalla: *prior tempore, potior iure.*[3] This means that in the context of priority disputes the first in time to be created prevails.

1 As the English common law has developed separately from systems that are strongly influenced by Roman law, I will use the Roman expressions instead of the common law expressions of 'charge' and 'mortgage'.

2 Under some bankruptcy laws, for instance the Dutch system, secured creditors are able to recover their debt as if there were no bankruptcy.

3 Ant. C. 8,18,3: 'If you receive a tract of land in pledge before it was encumbered to the State, as you were first in time, so you will be preferred by law.'

Owing to the Reception of Roman law, the first in time rule turns up explicitly in the civil code of several continental European countries.[4] Commonly, the principle of priority is expressed in the context of security rights. The range of application is actually wider in most countries, because the first in time rule is usually mentioned as a characteristic of rights *in rem* in general. The fact is, a real right is attached to property itself and can be enforced against anyone who encroaches upon it. So when successive interests in an asset have arisen, the one to whom a security interest was granted first may enforce his right without hindrance from any subsequent secured creditor.

This point of view – that is to say the first in time rule is a characteristic of rights in rem – is also held by the Pandectists, nineteenth-century German scholars of Roman law.[5] Their ambition to systematize the casuistic Pandects resulted in a wide application of the first in time rule, because under the Pandectists system not only the security rights *in rem* but also the rights *in rem* that serve to use property of someone else are covered by the first in time rule. That makes one wonder if the rule was originally supposed to be applied in conflicts between, for example, rights of usufruct and servitudes. This essay focuses on the original scope of application of the first in time rule. The question is in what context and how the first in time rule was applied according to Roman Law. Exposing the roots of the first in time rule by this comparative study will contribute to a better understanding of its modern application. To be able to answer the question regarding the original application of the rule, solutions to a number of conflicts between rights *in rem* will be scrutinized according to Roman law.[6] First, conflicts between security rights *in rem* will be discussed (paragraph two), followed by paragraph three in which solutions to conflicts between rights *in rem* of enjoyment will be examined. In the fourth paragraph the two sorts of rights in rem are combined, as Roman solutions to conflicts between rights of security and enjoyment will be inquired.

2. Security rights

As mentioned above, creditors could support the repayment of loans by taking security. Two means were at the creditor's disposal: personal security, that is by sureties, and proprietary security, which can be classified in *pignus* and *hypotheca*.[7] Since only creditors with a proprietary security interest obtained a strengthened position and were

4 For example Article 2425 Code civil français, §879 Bürgerliches Gezetsbuch and Article 21 of Bock 3 of the Dutch civil code.

5 See for instance Dernburg 1894, p. 95.

6 One should take into account that Roman law cannot be mentioned as such, as the Roman Empire has existed from 753 B.C. until 476 A.D. and the Byzantine Empire even until 1453. In the context of this essay Roman law refers to the code of laws compiled by order of the Emperor Justinian, because this Corpus Iuris has influenced the modern legal systems. Besides, this code is composed of writings of the Classical Roman law jurists.

7 It is a remarkable fact that the Ancient Rome practice preferred personal security to proprietary security interests. This can be explained by the strictness and rigidity of execution which was directed against the person and involved the debtor's – and thus also the surety's – whole patrimony. See Kaser 1971, p. 457.

less vulnerable in the event of the debtor's insolvency, this essay only deals with proprietary securities.[8]

Pignus and *hypotheca* are both real rights – protected by the same action[9] – in property of another. The difference is whether the possession of the thing was transferred to the creditor upon the constitution of the right (*pignus)* or it remained with the debtor (*hypotheca*).[10] A debtor is most likely unable to dispense with the encumbered things without harming his economical or personal interests. For that reason non possessory security interests were created frequently. The fact that the creditor is not in possession of the encumbered things, constitutes the danger of successive charging.[11] The debtor, as he is still the owner, is able to create a subsequent security interest in favour of another creditor, to whom then is given an unconditional right as well.[12] The question presents itself how the order of priority between the secured creditors should be determined. The Corpus Iuris makes clear that according to the principle *prior tempore potior iure,* the priority was settled in the order of the creation of the rights.[13] For this order of priority the day of the creation of the hypothecs was decisive. A day was considered to be an indivisible unit of time, so the days of creation were distinguished.[14] Two hypothecs given on the same day therefore shared the same rank.[15] The reason for this is the practicality that mostly the exact time of the creation is unknown. There is, however, no reason to let a creditor share the rank with a creditor who's right was created earlier on the same day when the order of creation is well known.[16] So in that case the first creditor – in accordance with the first in time rule – must be preferred over the subsequent one.

8 The oldest type that served to realize the purpose of giving real security is *fiducia*, which is the transfer of ownership for security. The legal types *pignus* and *hypotheca* have developed separately. When Justinian effaced the *mancipatio* as a mode for the transfer of ownership, the *fiducia* was changed into *pignus*. See Kaser 1975, p. 313.

9 The *action Serviana* was directed to the acquisition or reacquisition of possession from any possessor. See Kaser 1971, p. 472–473.

10 See Ulp. D. 13,7,9,2. One should realize that the transfer of possession could take place *constituto possessorio*, which means that the debtor retains the thing after the transfer. Pignus then appeared to be the same as hypotheca. This provides an explanation for the quote of Roman jurist Marcian, stated in D. 20,1,5,1 that the difference between *pignus* and *hypotheca* is only one of words.

11 At first, in the classical period, successive charging was impossible because the subsequent charge was recognized on condition that the first right of *pignus* was extinguished. See Gai. D. 20,1,5,2.

12 Although the subsequent creditor is protected by the *actio Serviana* as well, the action fails if a creditor with a prior *pignus* raises the *exceptio rei sibi ante pignoratae* (defence of prior *pignus)*. See Marci. D. 20,4,12 pr. and Mar. D. 44,2,19.

13 See Ant. C. 8,18,3.

14 See Paul. D. 2,12,8, supported by Windscheid 1862, p. 637.

15 See Paul. D. 13,7,20,1. The possessor of the property had *de facto* the stronger right as only he was able to sell it. The non-possessor's *actio Serviana* failed now the possessor could raise the exception 'You could have the property, if it had not been agreed that it should also be pledged to me'. See Ulp. D. 20,1,10.

16 This view is also supported by Dernburg 1864, p. 406.

The first in time rule was applied irrespective of whether the oldest creditor had a hypothec that extended to the entire patrimony of the debtor, a so called general hypothec, or a security interest that extended to a single asset, a special hypothec. In ancient Rome the creation of general hypothecs was common practise.[17] This could have led to the unreasonable situation in which a creditor, to whom a possessory security interest was given, was defeated by someone to whom was given a general hypothec before. The first creditor can sell the exact asset that was encumbered in favour of the subsequent creditor as well, even now the subsequent one has possession of the encumbered assets and even though he could have recovered his claim by selling any other asset that has not been subsequently encumbered.[18]

It should be mentioned that in the Ancient Roman legal practice very little conflicts occurred. The fact is that most creditors were fully aware of any preceding encumbrance. This is in the first place the result of the duty of the debtor to inform the creditor about the encumbered state. By neglecting his duty, he committed a *crimen stellionatus*, for which one could be heavily sentenced.[19] The deterrent effect of such penalties prevented the debtor from withholding from any encumbrance.

Though drawing up a letter of hypothecation was not a constitutive requirement, it was common practise to do so for matters of proof as a system of registration was lacking.[20] The Corpus Iuris however shows that these letters of hypothecation functioned poorly within scope of the publicity of preceding encumbrances.[21] It occurred that letters were antedated by creditors in order to obtain the position of first creditor.[22] To put a stop to the commission of fraud, Emperor Leo ordered that creditors who founded their security interest upon a document that was publicly executed – or upon a privately executed document that bore the signature of three witnesses, all of approved and honourable reputation – should be preferred.[23] This distinction between the ways of creation – on the one hand creditors who had recorded a security interest before a public authority (or three witnesses) and on the other hand secured creditors who did not – changed the fact that the order of priority was determined in order of the creation of the rights. Creditors,

17 See Pap. D. 20,1,1 pr. and Gai D. 20,1,15,1. Frequently such a security interest was given in addition to a special hypothec to strengthen the creditor's position. See Kaser 1971, p. 466.

18 Explicitly noted in Pap. D. 20,4,2. The creditors autonomy stems from Marci. D. 20, 5,8. The exception noted in Sev. and Ant. C. 8,14,2 – that is to say that the strictness of the rule should be relaxed so that a creditor shall not be deprived of that portion of the same property which was subsequently encumbered – is only applicable on the older creditor who had both a general and a special hypothec. Since the Middle Ages this provision has been known as the *beneficium excussionis realis*.

19 See Ulp. D. 13,7,36,1.

20 The fact that a hypothec could be created without a letter of hypothecation stems from Gai. D. 20,1,4. Scaevola confirms in D. 20,1,34,1 that the hypothec is not void when the letter has no date.

21 It occurred that the letter had no date or an incorrect one, or that the letter was lost. See Scae. D. 20,1,34,1, Mod. D. 48,10,28 and Paul. D. 44,2,30,1. As a result a debtor could have also been ignorant of the rights created by his legal predecessor.

22 See Mod. D. 48,10,28.

23 See Leo C. 8,18,11,1.

who had hypothecs created by a public document, were given priority over creditors with a privately created hypothec, even if the security interest of the last mentioned creditor was first created.[24]

Much of a bigger influence on the order of priority were the legal hypothecs that enjoyed the privilege of priority. These security interests developed during the post-classical age from preferential rights in favour of certain classes of creditors and were created by operation of law.[25] Among these the hypothec of the wife with regard to her claim for the dowry can be mentioned, as well as the hypothec of the state for taxes and contractual claims and the hypothec of the creditor whose money was spent for the preservation of a pledged property over this property.[26] The order of priority, which was settled according to the first in time rule, was greatly deprived of its value by these privileges of priority. A privileged hypothec ranked above all other conventional creditors as it took its rank not from its time of creation but from the law. The order of priority between the privileged secured creditors was determined by law as well.[27]

During the classical age conflicts of priority were settled according to the first in time rule.[28] The privileges of priority which increased considerably in the post-classical period as well as the preferential right for debt recorded before a public authority (Lex Leo) have however heavily impaired credit.[29] A creditor could not ascertain himself of the absence of any subsequent security interest that gained priority.

3. Rights of enjoyment

Property could not only be encumbered in favour of a creditor, but also in favour of a beneficiary[30] in such a way that its owner had to suffer certain interferences by the beneficiary or had to abstain interfering with the thing himself.[31] These rights of enjoyment, protected by actions *in rem*, involve the use or the taking of the fruits of

24 It should be mentioned that the creditor to whom this preferential right was detrimental had himself to blame since he could have created his right before a public authority as well.

25 See Kaser 1971, p. 466. These hypothecs could be both general and special.

26 See in that order Just. C. 8,18,12,4; Ant. C. 4,46,1 and Ulp. D. 20,4,5.

27 The fiscus takes priority as stems from Ant. C. 4,46,1, supported by Windscheid 1862, p. 648. The hypothec of the wife with regard to her claim for the dowry is preferred over the so called hypothecs for *versio im rem*, the hypothec of the creditor whose money was spent for the preservation of a pledged property. See Novelle 97,3. This conclusion is however not undisputed. See Dernburg 1864, p. 453–454.

28 With the exception of Sev. and Ant. C. 8,14,2 that shows that under certain circumstances the strictness of the rule should be relaxed. See footnote 18.

29 The different types of hypothecs in combination with the lack of a system of registration has led to the widely accepted conclusion that the Roman security law system hasn't come out as well as the other parts of the Roman legislation. See Kaser 1975, p. 313.

30 Beneficiary does not refer to a beneficiary of trust but to a person to whom a right of enjoyment was granted.

31 For the record, the distinction of restricted real rights in rights of enjoyment and rights of security is not of Roman origin as the Roman legislation was rather casuistic in its formulations.

property that is owned by another person. The principle rights of enjoyment, though not the only ones, were servitudes.[32] In Justinian's law the concept of servitudes was divided into real servitudes and personal servitudes.[33] Real servitudes can be defined as rights exercised over some land of which one was not the owner (the servient land), by a person in benefit of the land which they owned (the dominant land).[34] The servitude could only consist in the duty from the owner of the servient land to forbear or to abstain from doing something, and therefore not in a positive duty to do something.[35] Personal servitudes were rights not in benefit of land, but in benefit of a person.[36] The most common personal servitude was the right of *ususfructus* which can be defined as the right to use and enjoy the things of another, their substance remaining unimpaired.[37]

From the owner's point of view a difference between a servitude and a usufruct is the fact that when the owner has granted a servitude he can still enjoy the thing himself. He just has to suffer interference by the grantee. On the other hand if he granted a usufruct he must abstain from interfering with the thing himself as the exclusive right of enjoyment belongs to the grantee. This difference has to be taken into account when scrutinizing possible conflicts between rights of enjoyment.

The owner of land who has granted another a servitude, for example a right of passage or of driving cattle through a specific place, can certainly grant either of these rights to several persons through the same place.[38] The *Corpus Iuris* explicitly mentions that he can impose a similar servitude on the same land in favour of as many other persons as he wishes. Mostly, the owners of several dominant properties will not be at cross-purposes. They can for example pass over the servient land without hindrance from each other. It should be mentioned that the owner of the dominant property can grant the servitudes on different days or on different hours. It can be granted over the same place or on the same days during the same hours as well. It is however required that the servitude to be created can be exercised among the already existing servitudes. For example in case of a

32 Two other rights *in rem* vested in a non-owner are *emphyteusis* and *superficies*. The first mentioned was the grant of land on a long lease or in perpetuity upon the payment of a *canon*. Superficies is a right over land as well and originated in the grant of land for building purposes upon paying a rent as well. Both rights are protected by an *actio in rem*.

33 Marci. D. 8,1,1. This classification is not of classical origin. The personal servitudes were thought of separately and can be found in titles in the *Corpus Iuris* which are different from the ones that involve real servitudes. In fact, personal servitudes had little in common with the real servitudes.

34 In the classical period Gaius distinguished depending on their purpose between rustic praedial servitudes and urban servitudes. See G. 2,14.

35 See Pomp. D. 8,1,15,1.

36 Personal servitudes were therefore inevitably limited in duration, at longest for the life of the grantee. The right extinguished by his death. It was for the record a right *in rem* as much as a real servitude as it gave a right of using the encumbered thing irrespective of who its owner was.

37 Paul. D. 7,1,1. Among the right of *usufructus* as a personal servitude the right of *usus* can be mentioned.

38 Paul. D. 8,4,15. The same goes for the right of an aqueduct or to draw water in order that it may be conducted over the same place. See Ner. D. 8,3,2,1.

right to draw water, the right may be granted to several people as long as the supply of the water to be drawn is sufficient.[39]

The question presents itself how conflicts must be settled when the owner of dominant property despite of an insufficient water supply grants another right to draw water. One of the general requirements that can be derived from the nature of servitudes was that the exercise had to be possible perpetually and not merely for a limited time (*causa perpetua).*[40] So in case of water rights it is required that there is a continuous or continually recurrent supply of water. If there is not, the servitude does not meet the requirements for its creation. It seems that according to Roman law the grant of such a servitude – that is to say one that actually cannot be exercised, at least not without any detriment to another owner of dominant property – is simply void.

Besides, the Corpus Iuris shows that a subsequent servitude that either cannot be factually exercised, or as a result of its creation makes the exercise of an existing servitude impossible, cannot be granted.[41] A servitude that is created to the detriment of any owner of dominant property – as any owner cannot exercise his right anymore – shall be void. The person in favour of whom such a servitude was tried to be created, will have to manage with a claim for compensation.[42] Another explanation, for instance that this servitude is lawfully created but that this right cannot be exercised to the detriment of the other grantee, as their right was created first in time, must be rejected. The application of the first in time rule in the context of servitudes is not supported by the Corpus Iuris.

As mentioned above, the owner of the servient land can grant a similar servitude in favour of as many persons as he wishes as long as the right can factually be exercised by the owners of dominant properties. Yet it could occur that some of the beneficiaries quarrelled about the way or the time of exercising the servitude.[43] When this was the case, the order of priority between the beneficiaries had to be determined. Priority was not settled according to the first in time rule. In fact, by analogy with the rules of co-ownership in which each of the common owners had an undivided share, the owners of dominant properties could demand that the community be dissolved by the *iudicium communi dividendo* (the general partition action).[44] This did not necessarily result in

39 Ner. D. 8,3,2,2.

40 Paul. D. 8,2,28. See about this requirement Kaser 1971, p. 442–443. In the *ius commune* this requirement was disputed, it was widely accepted by the Pandectists though. See for example Windscheid 1862, p. 532 and Dernburg 1894, p. 586.

41 Pomp. D. 8,3,14 mentioning that a right of way and a watercourse through the same place are mutually exclusive.

42 This is supported by Windscheid 1862, p. 532, footnote 8. Should it be the case that this person nevertheless exercises the (what he believes to be lawfully created) servitude, the grantees are protected by the *actio confessoria*. Ulp. D. 8,5,10,1.

43 As mentioned above, the exercise could be restricted to certain days or hours to prevent conflicts.

44 Jul. D. 43,20,4. In this context the Corpus mentions this action as *utile* or *quasi* iudicium communi dividendo. Another solution is, of course, that they by *stipulation* regularize the exercise of the servitude, but only if they could come to an agreement.

the Praetor judging the use to one of the parties for which the other accepts compensation, the position of both parties could be regularized by the Praetor as well.[45] So the Praetor could restrain the owners of dominant land and determine how, at what times or which places, each party shall make use of the servitude. This solution, as the authoritative classic Roman jurists Julian and Ulpian argue, was based on reasonableness.[46]

As to the right of usufruct, it should be stated that the most common way of creating this right was by legacy.[47] In order to make it possible to provide maintenance for certain disinherited members of the family entitled to succession upon death, a *legatum usufructus* was given to them.[48] Now that a usufruct could be granted by legacy to several people, it is not surprising that conflicts between several usufructuaries can only be found in the part of the Roman casuistic legislation regarding inheritance matters.

As the usufructuaries, who have acquired the usufruct by inheritance, had equal rights with regard to the encumbered property, it is natural that the rules of co-ownership are by analogy applied to them as well. Any usufructuary was entitled to use the burdened thing and take its fruits independently, though respectfully, of the others. So when the usufructuaries quarrelled about the way of exercising the usufruct, any one of them could demand that the 'community' be dissolved by a partition action.[49]

When several people were granted the usufruct over the same property not by legacy but by contract, the analogy with co-ownership and the application of the partition act in this context is less justifiable.[50] A usufructuary to whom the actual exercise of the right was granted and the toleration of such exercise was promised, is most likely not willing to share the right of usufruct with those to whom a usufruct over the same property was subsequently created by contract.[51]

The Corpus Iuris shows that the owner may not create a subsequent usufruct over the same property because he may not interfere with the usufructuary or render the usufruct's condition worse.[52] If the owner nevertheless interferes with the usufructuary he will be liable to an action on the ground of fraud.[53] Although one cannot on this basis come to the conclusion that the creation of a subsequent usufruct is not permitted and therefore void, this explanation is rather plausible. After all, a usufructuary has the full

45 See Paul. D. 10,3,10,1 for the solution of adjudging to one party and Windscheid 1862 p. 428 for the solution to regularize.
46 See Ulp. D. 7,1,13,3 and Jul. D. 43,20,4.
47 Kaser 1971, p. 451.
48 Such a legacy was for example given to the widow, when the children inherited the property.
49 See Ulp. D. 7,1,13,1.
50 It was very well possible to create a usufruct by *traditio et patentia*, see Kaser 1971, p. 451, as well as, more commonly, by the transferor's reservation when transferring ownership of the thing.
51 It should be mentioned that successive creation does not lead to any conflict. A subsequently created usufruct could be exercised without hindrance after the first right was extinguished.
52 Ulp. D. 7,1,15,6.
53 See Ulp. D. 7,4,5,3 and Paul. D. 8,5,9 pr.

and exclusive right to use the burdened property and take its fruits. Someone else cannot be granted this exact same full and exclusive right, at least not without causing detriment to the first usufructuary. Besides, the owner cannot create any servitudes that negatively affect the usufructuary either.[54] There is no reason to assume that the owner can nonetheless create rights of enjoyments like usufructs that deprive the owner of his enjoyment to an even larger extent.[55] Again, a solution in accordance with the first in time rule in this context is not supported by the Corpus Iuris. In view of what has been stated above, it seems that a subsequent usufruct over the same property was void and could therefore not cause priority conflicts.[56]

4. Combination of rights of security and enjoyment

In practise, conflicts between a security right and a right of enjoyment particularly occurred when it had to be determined whether a secured creditor, who was about to sell the secured property, had to do so encumbered with the right of enjoyment or not. Until the moment of the sale, rights of enjoyment do not negatively affect the security interest of the creditor and could be exercised without any hindrance to the creditor. It would only be detrimental to the creditor if he must respect the right of enjoyment at the moment of the sale by selling encumbered property. For that reason the order of priority between a security interest and a right of enjoyment should be determined.

Several rights, both of security and enjoyment, could be created over the same property. It is beyond doubt that the owner of the property, after giving security, may still create rights of enjoyment over the same property in favour of someone else.[57] The opposite situation – creating a security interest after the creation of a right of enjoyment – was also very well possible.[58]

When both a usufruct and hypothec had been created over the same property, the idea of the first in time rule plays an important part in settling the priority when it comes to a forced sale. The Codex states that a right of usufruct remains unimpaired after the

54 This actually stems from the Coprus Iuris, see. Ulp. D. 7,1,15,7 and Paul. D. 7,1,16.

55 For the other rights of enjoyment, superficies and emphytheusis, goes the same. As a beneficiary of one of these rights has the full and exclusive use of the encumbered property, any right subsequently created over the same property must be considered void.

56 For the record it must be mentioned that this conclusion only applies to an identical subsequent usufruct. Considering the fact that a usufruct could be restricted in time (different to the limitation in duration of the life of the beneficiary), the invalidity does only extend to the overlapping time frames. So if a first usufruct was of limited duration, for example ten years, a subsequently created usufruct could not be valid until the first had been extinguished.

57 For example Pomp. D. 50,17,205 mentions that a servitude can be imposed upon land that already had been encumbered with a security right in favour of Treasury.

58 Sev. and Ant. C. 3,33,2 allows the owner to create a hypothec even now the usufructuary had the exclusive use of the property.

creation of a subsequent right of hypothec.[59] This means that the creditor can only sell the property encumbered with the usufruct. The usufructuary can exercise his right irrespective of who the owner of the property is. So when the ownership of the encumbered property is transferred, the transferee must abstain from interfering with the property.

When on the other hand the hypothec was first created, a subsequently created usufruct cannot prejudice the right of the creditor. The fact is, the Codex states in 8,14,15 that a debtor cannot prejudice the rights of creditors by either selling, donating, bequeathing or leaving under a trust the property pledged. Although creating a usufruct is not actually mentioned, it must be assumed that this restriction to the debtor also includes the creation of rights of enjoyment. The concerning edict expresses the principle of *droit de suite*[60], as the creditor can assert his right to the same.[61] There is no reason to assume that a creditor can assert his right against any transferee or donee, but would not be able to do so against a usufructuary. If the opposite were true, a debtor could completely undermine the creditor's security interest by creating one usufruct after another.

Since the right of usufruct gives the usufructuary the full and exclusive right to use and enjoy property, it is clear that the rights of a creditor will be prejudiced when property charged in his favour is subsequently encumbered by such a right. This situation could be different when, rather than a usufruct, a servitude is subsequently created. In fact, the question whether a creditor is prejudiced by the fact that the owner – and thus any possible auction buyer– must forbear or abstain from doing something is not quite simple to answer. It is a rather factual question and its answer depends on the nature and the content of the servitude.[62]

One could argue that if the creation of a servitude causes only a minor devaluation of the secured property, that is to say to this extent that the creditor can still recover his debt, this servitude remains valid in the event of the sale by the secured creditor. Although this view attempts to favour all those involved in the property as best one can, it runs into difficulties, because not until the moment the property has been sold will it be clear whether the proceeds are sufficient or not.

The maintenance, on the other hand, of the servitude in the event of the sale by the creditor, would not do justice to the right of hypothec of the creditor. He should be able

59 It seems that the immediate cause for this judgement was the intention of a creditor to sell the property unencumbered with the right of usufruct, against which the usufructuary took action by requesting the Praetor to secure the usufruct.

60 The French term *droit de suite* denotes the right of a creditor to pursue the debtor's property into the hands of third persons for the enforcement of his claim.

61 Dioc. and Max. C. 8,14,15.

62 It goes without saying that a servitude of allowing the dripping of rainwater on the roof of a neighbour prejudices the right of the owner of servient property to a greater extent than a servitude to conduct or draw water.

to sell the property the way it was when the hypothec was created. When taking security for the repayment of a certain loan, a creditor cannot be expected to anticipate possible servitudes to be created in the future.

The more plausible opinion on the subject is what is called by the Pandectists the 'strict view', meaning that any servitude subsequently created, no matter to what extent the prejudice to the property may be, must yield to the hypothec when the creditor sells the property.[63] The strictness of this view lies in the strict application of the first in time rule. The moment both rights conflict, which is the case when the creditor sells the property, the right first created is preferred over the right subsequently created, no matter its content or nature.

The application of the first in time rule leads to the result that, in this last conflict to be discussed, the servitude, that was created before security was given over the same property, will be intact when the creditor sells the property. As the beneficiary of the servitude was the first in time, the creditor must endure his right by selling the property encumbered with the servitude.

5. Conclusion

As discussed in the above, the first in time rule was applied in the context of security rights *in* rem. Paragraph two states that the order of priority between secured creditors was determined in accordance with the first in time rule, no matter whether the security interests consisted in general or special hypothecs. The creditor to whom a hypothec was given at an earlier point in time, was preferred over the creditor to whom a hypothec was subsequently given over the same property.

In the course of the empire, after the classic Roman age, two exceptions to the first in time rule appeared. The first one can be described as a measure by Emperor Leo to remedy the lack of publicity, by preferring creditors who had recorded their right before a public authority. This measure was supposed to encourage the creation of security interests by authentic document. The other exception to the principle of priority, was the fact that some hypothecs, created in favour of some classes of creditors, enjoyed the privilege of priority. These hypothecs were created and ranked by operation of law. As a result of both exceptions it could occur that a hypothec was created first in time, but in spite of this, had to give priority to another creditor.

As discussed in paragraph three, conflicts between several beneficiaries of rights of enjoyment are not settled according to the first in time rule. Either these conflicts, for example two usufructuaries entitled to use the same property, could not occur because

63 See Dernburg 1864, p. 149, who is in the belief that he is supported by Windscheid 1862, p. 625. Windscheid, however, does not give his opinion on hypothec versus servitude conflicts, he just speaks in broad terms about the application of the priority rule.

any subsequent right of usufruct is assumed to be void, or these conflicts are settled in a different way, that is according to the rules of co-ownership, by which each of the beneficiaries was able to request a partition action (*iudicium communi dividendo*).

In the situation in which two sorts of rights *in rem* – both rights of security and enjoyment – were created over the same property, the first in time rule settled the conflict too. As stated in paragraph four, a creditor can sell the property the way it was when the security interest was created. In accordance with the first in time rule the creditor can sell the property unencumbered with subsequent rights of enjoyment.

The above mentioned leads to the conclusion that under Roman law the first in time rule was applied in conflicts of rights *in rem* in which at least one security right took part. When a security right had a conflicting interest with either another security right or any right of enjoyment, the first in time rule settled the order of priority.

Bibliography

Dernburg 1864
Dernburg, H., *Das Pfandrecht nach den Grundsätzen des heutigen römischen Rechts. Zweiter Band,* Leipzig: Hirzel, 1864.

Dernburg 1894
Dernburg, H., *Pandekten. Erster Band: Allgemeiner Theil und Sachenrecht,* Berlin: Müller, 1894.

Kaser 1971
Kaser, M., *Das römische Privatrecht I: das altrömische, das vorklassische und klassische Recht,* München: Beck, 1971.

Kaser 1975
Kaser, M., *Das römische Privatrecht II: die nachklassischen entwicklungen,* München: Beck, 1975.

Windscheid 1862
Windscheid, B., *Lehrbuch des Pandektenrechts, Erster Band,* Düsseldorf: Verlagshandlung van Julius Buddeus, 1862.

Björn Hoops*

PAUL KRUGERBRUG REVISITED: STATE ACTION WITH AN EXCESSIVE IMPACT ON PROPERTY RIGHTS FROM A COMPARATIVE PERSPECTIVE

1. Introduction

When the State takes away property rights on land from a company in order to use the land in the public interest, the business activities of the company, insofar as they depend upon the property rights, have to be halted. The company will have to resume its business activities somewhere else. However, it will receive just and equitable compensation. There are, however, other forms of state action affecting the exercise of property rights that do not lead to expropriation in the sense of a transfer of property rights, but equally threaten the economic viability of a company.

One example would be the plan to build a new non-moveable bridge in the municipality of Utrecht, The Netherlands. The private limited company Liesbosch B.V. (*Besloten vennootschap met beperkte aansprakelijkheid*; hereinafter referred to as: Liesbosch) was operating a shipyard in the municipality of Nieuwegein in the Dutch province of Utrecht. At the shipyard, Liesbosch *inter alia* produced and repaired ships by order of companies that belonged to its corporate group or other companies. To deliver the ships Liesbosch made use of the *Merwedekanaal* (Merwede Canal) that connected the shipyard through two locks to the *Amsterdam-Rijnkanaal* (Amsterdam-Rhine Canal), which links the harbour of Amsterdam to the industrial *Ruhr* region in Germany. On their way through the canal, ships with a width of 12 to 14 metres had to pass the drawbridge *Paul Krugerbrug* (Paul Kruger Bridge), located in the west of Utrecht. In the 1970s, the municipality of Utrecht was planning to build a new tram line from Utrecht to Nieuwegein. The new tram was envisaged to run over the Paul Kruger Bridge. To improve traffic security and reduce costs the municipality of Utrecht decided to replace the drawbridge with a non-moveable bridge. On 7 March 1980 *Rijkswaterstaat*, the Dutch Highways Agency, granted the municipality permission to remove the old drawbridge and to build the new non-moveable bridge. The new bridge would only have an altitude of 3.63 metres. The bigger type of ships that Liesbosch built or repaired, however, could have a height of up to 6.85 metres.

* LL.M., PhD Candidate and Lecturer, Faculty of Law, University of Groningen.

The plan to build the new bridge regulated the property rights on the land on which the bridge was to be built. However, it affected the property rights of Liesbosch as well. Liesbosch could no longer make (profitable) use of their land to build or repair larger ships without making very costly adjustments to the available infrastructure. As the turnover of the company largely depended upon ships of that type, this state action threatened the economic viability of Liesbosch. The *Afdeling rechtspraak van de Raad van State* (ARRvS; Judicial Division of the Dutch Council of State; hereinafter referred to as: Judicial Division) held in two judgments that Liesbosch was entitled to compensation for this excessive form of state action.

In this contribution, it is analysed from a comparative perspective what constitutes the legal foundation of this claim to compensation under current Dutch and German law and how this legal foundation has evolved under Dutch law since the *Paul Krugerbrug* jurisprudence. Having described the judgments of the Judicial Division on this case, I discuss how this excessive state action would be classified under Dutch and German law. Subsequently, a section is dedicated to the obligation to take measures under Dutch and German law that prevent or compensate the damage caused by the state action. I first discuss the legal basis of the claim and the role of the administrative body that has taken the decision that affects the property. I then analyse what kind of measures have to be taken to prevent or compensate the inflicted damage and discuss the legal criteria to which the claim to such measures is subject. Lastly, I describe the judicial protection of the holder of property rights. This contribution, however, does not contain an analysis of the calculation of the amount of compensation. I conclude the contribution with a brief comparison of the protection from expropriation and the protection from such excessive state action.

2. The *Paul Krugerbrug* judgments of the Judicial Division

2.1. The Paul Krugerbrug I judgment

On 12 January 1982, the Judicial Division passed the first of two *Paul Krugerbrug* judgments that shaped the rules on compensation for state action affecting property rights in the Netherlands. The court revoked the permission granted to the municipality, considering that it had not been reasonable for *Rijkswaterstaat* to grant the permission.[1] The court justified this conclusion as follows. During the court proceedings, the Minister acknowledged that before *Rijkswaterstaat* granted the permission, the decision-making body had been of the opinion that under Dutch law, Liesbosch had a right to receive compensation for the harm that it would suffer as a result of the permission. In spite thereof, *Rijkswaterstaat* granted the permission without determining the amount of the compensation and even without ascertaining the damage that Liesbosch would suffer. On the contrary, specialists estimated the damage, and the municipality determined the amount of compensation long after the permission had been granted. On 10 March 1981, the municipality had offered Liesbosch and its corporate group compensation of

1 ARRvS, Judgment of 12 January 1982, AB 1982, 299.

2.208 million guilders (~€1 million), equalling 40% of the estimated total damage of 5.5 million guilders (~€2.5 million). This led the Judicial Division to the conclusion that *Rijkswaterstaat* had not sufficiently respected Liesbosch's warranted interest to know before the permission was granted what amount would be awarded as compensation. Having justified its conclusion, the court added that the method to calculate the amount of compensation had to be clarified and explained better.

The court's conclusion that it was not reasonable to grant the permission implies that granting the permission was contrary to the prohibition of arbitrary administrative action.[2] This judgment first shows that the administrative body must ascertain how much harm its decision would cause and take this harm into account when balancing the relevant interests.[3] Furthermore, if a person has a claim to compensation as a result of this harm, this person has a right to know before the administrative body takes that decision which amount will be awarded. The judgment indicates that should the administrative body not award compensation and notify the person in such a case, the decision will violate the prohibition of arbitrary administrative action.[4] The judgment, however, remains silent on the criteria to which the claim to compensation is subject.

2.2. The Paul Krugerbrug II judgment

Three months after the *Paul Krugerbrug I* judgment, on 7 April 1982, *Rijkswaterstaat* again granted a permission to the municipality of Utrecht. The permission also included, as specialists had advised, the compensation of 40% of the estimated damage, 6.14 million guilders (~€2.79 million), that Liesbosch would suffer as a result of the permission. *Rijkswaterstaat* thus respected Liesbosch's right to know before the permission was granted which amount would be awarded. Liesbosch, however, did not regard the awarded amount as sufficient compensation and feared that, without sufficient compensation, the company would no longer be viable. Therefore, Liesbosch lodged an appeal against the permission with the Judicial Division. On 22 November 1983, the Judicial Division delivered the *Paul Krugerbrug II* judgment and, again, revoked the permission, having concluded that the permission was contrary to the prohibition of arbitrary administrative action.[5]

In the beginning, however, the court clarified that in general, *Rijkswaterstaat* could reasonably grant the permission after balancing the advantages of the non-moveable bridge against its disadvantages, including the harm done to Liesbosch. This shows that the permission was not arbitrary in the sense that it was disproportionate or otherwise

2 Tjepkema 2010, p. 107. Today, this principle is codified in Article 3:4(2) of the General Administrative Law Act (*Algemene wet bestuursrecht*).

3 De Graaf & Marseille 2014, No. 1031.

4 Tjepkema 2010, p. 107; Van den Broek 1999; In an earlier judgment, a decision of an administrative body that inflicted excessive damage upon certain persons was held to be valid because compensation was awarded. See: ARRvS, Judgment of 15 December 1981, AB 1982, 298.

5 ARRvS, Judgment of 22 November 1983, AB 1984, 154.

based upon a flawed overall balancing of interests. The arbitrariness rather followed from the percentage of the damage that Liesbosch would have to bear. The court first reiterated the possibly fatal economic consequences of the permission. The court considered that the normal entrepreneurial risk did not entail that an administrative body could inflict such damage upon Liesbosch without any compensation. Therefore, *Rijkswaterstaat* had to award fair (*billijk*) compensation. The court gave a few indications as to what fair compensation means. It considered that the transport policy of the municipality was foreseeable. Furthermore, when determining the compensation, *Rijkswaterstaat* had to take account of all circumstances of the case, e.g. the economic position of Liesbosch after the new non-moveable bridge has been constructed. It did not take into account the economic ties between Liesbosch and its corporate group because Liesbosch was an independent economic entity. The Judicial Division concluded that given these circumstances, 80% of the damage had to be compensated and that *Rijkswaterstaat* could not reasonably decide only to award compensation that amounted to 40% of the damage.

The *Paul Krugerbrug II* judgment shows that proportionate and, therefore, generally lawful state action may be set aside by the courts as unlawful if compensation is not awarded to the holder of affected property rights that has a claim to compensation.[6] From this insight, it follows that the administrative body is obliged to award compensation in such cases.[7] Unlike in the *Paul Krugerbrug I* judgment, the Judicial Division also sketches the criteria to which the claim to compensation is subject. It considered that the damage that Liesbosch would suffer is not a materialisation of the normal entrepreneurial risk and should, therefore, at least partially be compensated. The normal entrepreneurial risk thus seems to be one of the criteria to which the claim to compensation is subject.[8] This consideration would further suggest that damage that follows from the normal entrepreneurial risk does not need to be compensated.

3. Classification of the state measure

3.1. No expropriation

As the permission granted by *Rijkswaterstaat* entailed that Liesbosch could no longer use its property for running a profitable shipyard, it threatened the economic viability of Liesbosch's undertaking. One could state with some justification that this permission has a quasi-expropriatory effect, *i.e.* an (physical rather than legal) impact on the property rights of Liesbosch that comes close to, or even equals, the effects of an expropriation. Despite this effect, the Judicial Division does not classify the permission as expropriation. The reason is that under Dutch law, the severity of the impact of state action on property rights is no longer[9] relevant to the definition of expropriation (*onteigening*) in terms of

6 Tjepkema 2010, p. 107; Schlössels 2002; De Graaf & Marseille 2014, No. 1031.

7 Tjepkema 2010, p. 108 *et seq*.

8 Tjepkema 2010, p. 109.

9 See about the historical development of the term expropriation: Van Zundert 1980, p. 121.

Article 14(1) of the Dutch Constitution, which is the Basic Law of 1983 (*Grondwet*; Gw). Instead, expropriation is defined as the transfer of property rights from the expropriatee to another entity in order for the property rights to be used in the public interest.[10] Therefore, under Dutch law, a formal criterion applies, namely the transfer of the property rights, and not a substantive criterion that is based upon the intensity of the impact of the state action. The plan to build the bridge and its effects on the property rights thus do not constitute expropriation.

Until 1981, the plan to build the non-moveable bridge on the basis of the Lower Saxonian Road Act would have qualified as expropriation (*Enteignung*) in the jurisprudence of the German Federal Supreme Court (*Bundesgerichtshof*; BGH). The BGH distinguished between expropriation for which compensation had to be awarded and social restrictions to property (*Sozialbindung*) that did not need to be compensated.[11] Whether or not state action qualified as expropriation depended upon the impact of the measure. The more the measure (physically or legally) affected the use and enjoyment of property, the more likely it was that the measure would qualify as expropriation.[12] The BGH would have classified the plan that includes the non-moveable bridge as expropriation because it threatened the existence of the Liesbosch's undertaking by cutting off the way for larger vessels to the canal linking Liesbosch to its clients.[13]

In 1981, the famous *Naßauskiesung* Decision of the German Federal Constitutional Court (*Bundesverfassungsgericht*; BVerfG) clarified the dogmatic structure of Article 14 of the German Constitution, which is the Basic Law of 23 May 1949 (*Grundgesetz*; GG). The BVerfG considered that state action could only constitute expropriation in terms of Article 14(3) GG if it fully or partially deprived a person of their property rights.[14] The BVerfG has ever since held consistently that even if the impact of the measure on the property is quasi-expropriatory, the measure would not turn into expropriation.[15] Like under Dutch law, a formal criterion applies, and the plan to build the bridge would not constitute expropriation.

10 Elzinga, De Lange & Hoogers 2014, p. 443; Den Drijver-van Rijckevorsel *et al.* 2013, p. 1.

11 BVerfG, Decision of 15 July 1981, NJW 1982, 745, 748; see, for instance, BGH, Judgment of 22 May 1980, NJW 1980, 2705.

12 Külpmann 2000, p. 16.

13 BGH, Judgment of 7 July 1980, NJW 1980, 2703, 2704. Alternatively, the permission may also have qualified as expropriation because it reduced the value of the property significantly. The Judicial Division, however, did not deal with this issue. Cf. BGH, Judgment of 11 January 1979, NJW 1979, 1043, 1044; BGH, Judgment of 2 July 1959, NJW 1959, 1776, 1777.

14 BVerfG, Decision of 15 July 1981, NJW 1982, 745, 748. In the most recent jurisprudence, expropriation is defined as a state measure that is intended to deprive a person partially or fully of their property rights in order for the property to be used for a specific public task. See: BVerfG, Judgment of 17 December 2013, NVwZ 2014, 211, 213. There is a lively debate in the German literature on the definition of expropriation, which falls outside the scope of this contribution: Cf. Riedel 2012, p. 93 *et seq.*

15 BVerfG, Decision of 2 March 1999, NJW 1999, 2877, 2877 *et seq.*

3.2. *State action with an impact on property rights*

The plan to build the bridge legally affects the property rights on the land on which the bridge was to be built. Under Dutch law, one may classify the plan to build the bridge as a restriction to property (*beperking*) in terms of Article 14(3) Gw as it determines the use of the land.[16] The property rights of Liesbosch themselves are not regulated, but physically affected. As the *Paul Krugerbrug II* shows, this impact on the property rights of Liesbosch may have to be compensated as a(n indirect) result of the plan.

Under German law, the plan to build the non-moveable bridge has to be classified as the definition of the scope and the limits of property rights (*Inhalts- und Schrankenbestimmung*) in terms of Article 14(1), 2nd sentence, GG. Such state action refers to the abstract and general definition of the rights and obligations of the holders of property rights.[17] It not only includes parliamentary statutes, but also abstract and general norms enacted by administrative bodies.[18] Through the plan the administrative body applies such abstract and general norms and shapes the rights and obligations of the holders of property rights. The plan therefore also constitutes a definition of the scope and the limits of property rights on the land on which the bridge was to be built.[19] Under German law, the physical impact on the property rights of Liesbosch is classified and may have to be compensated as consequences of the plan.

To avoid confusion between the legal regulation of the property rights on the land on which the bridge was to be built and the physical impact on the property rights of Liesbosch, let us denote the plan to build the bridge as state action with an impact on property rights (hereinafter also referred to as: state action).

3.3. *State action with an excessive impact on property rights*

The Dutch *Paul Krugerbrug* jurisprudence indicates that the permission granted by *Rijkswaterstaat* imposed so excessive a burden upon Liesbosch that the State had to compensate the suffered harm. However, given the advantages of the new bridge, the Judicial Division stressed that the *Rijkswaterstaat* could reasonably grant the permission. The permission was thus state action with an excessive impact on property rights that only had to be set aside as no compensation had been awarded. In the next two subsections I analyse how German and Dutch law integrate into their legal system this kind of state action.

16 Cf. Elzinga, De Lange & Hoogers 2014, p. 443.

17 BVerfG, Decision of 14 July 1981, BVerfGE 58, 137, 144.

18 Von Arnauld 2002, p. 400; Külpmann 2000, p. 108.

19 See, for instance, on the provisions of a binding land-use plans in terms of the Federal Building Code (*Baugesetzbuch*): BVerfG, Decision of 22 February 1999, NVwZ 1999, 979, 980; BVerfG, Decision of 30 November 1988, BVerfGE 79, 174, 191 *et seq.* The actual construction of the bridge implements the plan and therefore also falls under Article 14(1), 2nd sentence, GG; see: Külpmann 2000, p. 109.

3.3.1. Dutch law

Under Dutch law, state action with an impact on property rights has to comply with general statutory norms and the general principles of sound administration (*algemene beginselen van behoorlijk bestuur*).[20] If state action complies with these norms and principles, it will be lawful. Persons whose property rights are affected will not have any right to compensation.

If it does not comply with these norms, state action will be unlawful. In particular, state action must comply with Article 3:4(2) of the General Administrative Law Act (Awb). It provides that the disadvantages arising from state action must not be disproportionate in relation to its goals. Otherwise, the state action would be disproportionate and, therefore, unlawful. I refer to this form of disproportionate state action as generally excessive state action. This term must be distinguished from individually excessive state action (hereinafter also referred to as: state action with an individually excessive impact on property rights), which refers to state action that imposes excessive burdens upon a single or small group of persons that are, however, not disproportionate in relation to its goals. This follows from the jurisprudence of the Judicial Division (since 1994: *Afdeling bestuursrechtspraak van de Raad van State*; ABRvS). The Judicial Division first recognised the principle *égalité devant les charges publiques* (equality of citizens before charges levied by the State) as forming part of Dutch law in the *Van Vlodrop* judgment of 1997. This principle forms the general basis of a claim for compensation for individually excessive state action, and administrative bodies have to apply this principle to its own actions in order to determine whether or not compensation has to be awarded.[21] In that judgment, the Judicial Division still found Article 3:4(2) Awb to form the basis of that principle.[22] Since 2003, however, the Judicial Division has consistently separated the proportionality test in terms of Article 3:4(2) Awb from compensation for individually excessive state action on the basis of *égalité devant les charges publiques*.[23]

In the literature, some scholars advocate that the consequence of this distinction is that compensation in money, in principle, cannot turn generally excessive state action into proportionate and, therefore, lawful state action.[24] In some judgments on large projects, however, the Judicial Division held that the proportionality of state action was contingent upon the existence of a compensation scheme.[25] It is uncertain whether this

20 Article 3:1(2) Awb clarifies that in particular the principle of prudent administration (Article 3:2 Awb) and the principle of proportionality (Article 3:4(2) Awb) not only apply to administrative decisions (*besluit*), such as the permission, but to all actions of administrative bodies.

21 ABRvS, Judgment of 6 May 1997, ECLI:NL:RVS:1997:AA6762, AB 1997, 229.

22 ABRvS, Judgment of 6 May 1997, ECLI:NL:RVS:1997:AA6762, AB 1997, 229.

23 ABRvS, Judgment of 12 November 2003, ECLI:NL:RVS:2003:AN7851, AB 2004, 95; ABRvS, Judgment of 8 November 2006, ECLI:NL:RVS:2006:AZ1762, AB 2007, 252.

24 Schueler 2002, p. 114; De Graaf, Comment on ABRvS, Judgment of 15 December 2004, ECLI:NL:RVS:2004:AR7552,AB 2005, 67. Differing: Hennekens 2000. Cf. Tjepkema 2010, p. 547.

25 ABRvS, Judgment of 29 December 2004, ECLI:NL:RVS:2004:AR8375, 2.4.5; ABRvS, Judgment of 26 September 2007, ECLI:NL:RVS:2005:BB4297, 2.12.

consideration merely requires the administrative body to provide *ex ante* for a remedy in cases where state action has an individually excessive impact[26] or whether the compensation scheme was necessary to tip the balance in favour of the project. Furthermore, other scholars defend that compensation in money can play a role in the framework of the proportionality test.[27] All this does not apply to measures that prevent disadvantages or restore the property. It is generally accepted that they can be weighed in favour of the state action.[28]

The permission to build the new non-moveable bridge in the *Paul Krugerbrug* jurisprudence does not constitute generally excessive state action. The Judicial Division highlighted that the advantages of the bridge were of such weight that the *Rijkswaterstaat* could reasonably grant the permission. This means that the new bridge was not generally excessive. It was, however, individually excessive because it caused so much damage to an individual entrepreneur, Liesbosch, that the decision became unlawful without compensation being granted.

3.3.2. German law

In German law, the BVerfG created a dogmatic system that divides state action with an impact on property rights into three groups. The first group consists of regulatory measures that comply with all relevant norms. That in particular means that the measure serves the public good and complies with the principle of proportionality[29] as well as the principle of equal treatment. This state action is valid and does not require any kind of compensation.[30]

The second group refers to state action that does not comply with relevant norms. Particularly, state action that erodes the core of property rights, for instance the private use of the property and the power to dispose of the property, is unconstitutional.[31] Furthermore, state action that not only in particular cases of hardship contravenes the principle of proportionality or the principle of equal treatment is also unconstitutional.[32] Besides, compensation in money cannot tip the balance in favour of the measure or take

26 Tjepkema 2010, p. 548.

27 Van Ravels, Comment on ABRvS, Judgment of 8 November 2006, ECLI:NL:RVS:2006:AZ1762, AB 2007/252.

28 See, for instance, ABRvS, Judgment of 9 July 2003, ECLI:NL:RVS:2003:AH9396.

29 The proportionality test consists of three steps, namely suitability, necessity and proportionality in the narrow sense. Proportionality in the narrow sense requires that the disadvantages of the expropriation do not outweigh substantially the benefits of the implementation of the project. See: Riedel 2012, p. 218, with more references.

30 BVerfG, Decision of 15 September 2011, NVwZ 2012, 429, 430; BVerfG, Decision of 2 March 1999, NJW 1999, 2877, 2878.

31 BVerfG, Decision of 15 September 2011, NVwZ 2012, 429, 430; BVerfG, Decision of 2 March 1999, NJW 1999, 2877, 2878.

32 BVerfG, Decision of 15 September 2011, NVwZ 2012, 429, 430; BVerfG, Decision of 2 March 1999, NJW 1999, 2877, 2879.

away the discriminatory character of the measure,[33] whereas material measures that prevent disadvantages or restore the property can.[34] As does state action that violates Article 3:4(2) Awb in Dutch law, this form of state action has so severe disadvantages that it cannot be justified at all. They can therefore be classified as generally excessive state action.

The plan to build the new non-moveable bridge in the *Paul Krugerbrug* scenario would not fall under this category. The construction of the bridge is proportionate and complies with the principle of equal treatment. Yet, it imposes an excessive burden upon an individual entity, Liesbosch. Under German law, this particular case of hardship turns the valid state action into a definition of the scope and the limits of property that requires equalisation (*ausgleichspflichtige Inhalts- und Schrankenbestimmung*).[35] The Basic Law obliges the legislator to add an equalisation scheme to the statutory basis of the state action in order to maintain the proportionality of the measure and avoid burdens that are contrary to the principle of equal treatment in such cases of hardship.[36] Should the legislator fail to enact such a scheme, the statutory basis of the state action will be unconstitutional and, if the BVerfG sees fit, will be declared invalid.[37] Judges could obviously set aside the state action, *in casu* the plan to build the non-moveable bridge. As does Dutch law, German constitutional law classifies the plan to build the non-moveable bridge as state action with an individually excessive impact on property rights. Furthermore, German law also foresees measures that relieve the disadvantages caused to Liesbosch. An important difference is that under German law, the legal problem is solved within the constitutional framework of the property clause. Dutch law, by contrast, addresses this problem in a general framework applicable to all forms of state action.

In the jurisprudence of the BGH, the action for compensation on the basis of an expropriatory infringement (*enteignender Eingriff*) also provides a remedy for cases of state action with an individually excessive impact on property rights. This compensation does not have a statutory basis, but developed in the case law of the BGH. The action is founded on the principle of individual sacrifice (*Aufopferungsgedanke*) in terms of §§74, 75 of the Introduction to the General State Laws for the Prussian States (*Allgemeines Landrecht für die preußischen Staaten*).[38] The compensation serves to equalise the unusual sacrifice (*Sonderopfer*) that an otherwise lawful infringement of property in terms of Article 14(1) GG directly imposes upon the holder of property rights.[39] The

33 BVerfG, Decision of 15 September 2011, NVwZ 2012, 429, 430; BVerfG, Decision of 2 March 1999, NJW 1999, 2877, 2879; Neumann, in: Stelkens/Bonk/Sachs, VwVfG, §74, No. 183.

34 See, for instance, Neumann, in: Stelkens/Bonk/Sachs, VwVfG, §74, No. 167.

35 Cf. Kischel 2003, p. 604 *et seq.*

36 BVerfG, Decision of 15 September 2011, NVwZ 2012, 429, 430.

37 BVerfG, Decision of 2 March 1999, NJW 1999, 2877, 2879.

38 BGH, Judgment of 29 March 1984, NJW 1984, 1876, 1877.

39 BGH, Judgment of 10 February 2005, NJW 2005, 1363; Külpmann 2000, p. 84 *et seq.*

scope of applicability of this action and whether or not Liesbosch could successfully make use of this action are analysed below.

3.3.3. Visualisation of the approaches to excessive state action

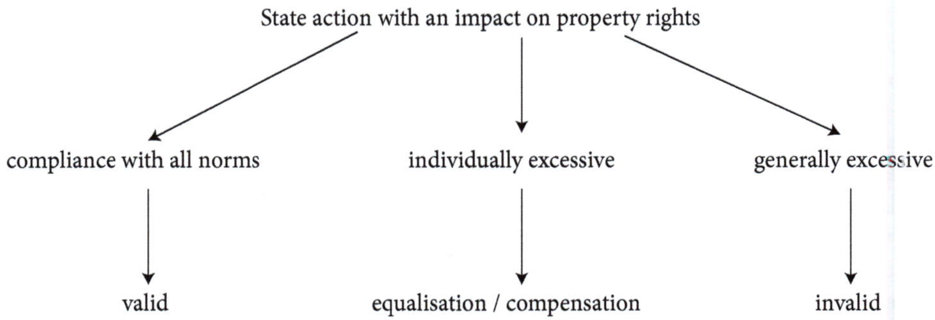

4. The obligation to take preventive measures and to pay compensation in money

4.1. Legal basis and the administrative decision to take equalising measures

4.1.1. Dutch law

On 31 January 2013, Title 4.5 of the Awb was promulgated, which is a codification of the current rules on compensation. This Title contains a set of statutory rules on the compensation of individual and excessive damage that a person suffers as a result of the lawful exercise of state power or the lawful fulfilment of a state task.[40] However, as the Title has yet to come into force, Dutch law does not provide for a comprehensive statutory compensation scheme, and Liesbosch could not invoke it. What follows, describes Dutch law as it is before Title 4.5 Awb comes into force.

Some statutes contain specific provisions on compensation for individually excessive state action to property.[41] Some administrative bodies adopt policy rules (*beleidsregel*) that provide for compensation in such cases. In the policy rule, the administrative body determines how it will meet its obligation to award compensation. This policy rule, of course, must still comply with higher norms. There is a policy rule that would be applicable to the *Paul Krugerbrug* scenario today, which is the Policy Rule on Compensation Infrastructure and Environmental Affairs 2014 (*Beleidsregel nadeelcompensatie Infrastructuur en Milieu 2014*). According to Article 2(1) of that policy rule, the Minister will award compensation to Liesbosch if the Minister or a

40 Article 4:126(1) Awb.

41 See, in particular, Article 6.1 of the Spatial Planning Act (*Wet ruimtelijke ordening*).

representative of the Minister does harm to Liesbosch in the exercise of their powers and Liesbosch should not bear the harm.

In the absence of a specific statutory basis for compensation, the claim to compensation must be based upon other sources of law. Until 1997, the competent administrative body had to decide upon whether compensation would be awarded for individually excessive, but otherwise lawful state action when taking the decision on the substance.[42] This decision is called a dependent decision on damages (*onzelfstandig schadebesluit*) because the decision on the damages was linked to the decision on the substance.[43] In line with the Judicial Division's jurisprudence in the *Paul Krugerbrug* case, the whole decision, including the decision on the substance, would otherwise be arbitrary.[44] The affected person had to lodge an appeal against that decision, and judges could set aside the unlawful decision in its entirety.[45] Otherwise, no compensation could be awarded. After the introduction of the Awb, the applicable norm in such cases was Article 3:4(2) Awb,[46] whereas the criteria for compensation were based upon the principle *égalité devant les charges publiques*.[47] This might lead to confusion because Article 3:4(2) Awb accommodated both the test whether state action is generally excessive and the test whether it is individually excessive.

In 1997, the Judicial Division delivered its judgment in the *Van Vlodrop* case. In that case, the Minister of Housing, Spatial Planning and the Environment (Minister van Volkshuisvesting, Ruimtelijke Ordening en Milieubeheer) altered its policy rules on the disposal of photographic chemical waste, which severely affected the business of Van Vlodrop B.V. Van Vlodrop B.V. requested compensation for this amendment. The Minister refused to award compensation. They declared a complaint inadmissible as the refusal to award compensation was not a justiciable decision, which means that Van Vlodrop could not lodge an appeal against the decision with the administrative courts. The Judicial Division set aside this decision and held that the decision upon whether or not to award compensation was a justiciable decision.[48] Thereby, the Judicial Division introduced the independent decision on compensation (*zelfstandig nadeelcompensatiebesluit*). This means that even if the affected person does not lodge any appeal against the decision on the substance, they can still request compensation and lodge an

42 De Graaf & Marseille 2014, No. 1031 *et seq.*

43 De Graaf & Marseille 2014, No. 1032.

44 De Graaf & Marseille 2014, No. 1031.

45 De Graaf & Marseille 2014, No. 1031 *et seq.*

46 Parliamentary History Awb I, p. 212; Van den Broek 1999, p. 1; Van Buuren, in: T&C Algemene wet bestuursrecht, Art. 3:4 Awb; ABRvS, Judgment of 27 August 2003, ECLI:NL:RVS:2003:AI1440, JB 2003/289.

47 Van Buuren, in: T&C Algemene wet bestuursrecht, Art. 3:4 Awb; ABRvS, Judgment of 6 May 1997, ECLI:NL:RVS:1997:AA6762, AB 1997, 229; ABRvS, Judgment of 8 November 2006, ECLI:NL:RVS:2006:AZ1762, AB 2007, 252.

48 ABRvS, Judgment of 6 May 1997, ECLI:NL:RVS:1997:AA6762, AB 1997, 229.

appeal against a decision that includes no or too little compensation.[49] Equally, the administrative body, in principle, does not need to decide upon compensation when taking the decision on the substance, but can postpone that decision.[50] However, the administrative body is obliged to take a decision on compensation when taking the decision on the substance if the harm that is projected to be done is so severe that the administrative body could not reasonably take the decision without awarding compensation.[51]

In the *Van Vlodrop* case, however, the Judicial Division held that the complaint of Van Vlodrop B.V. had to be declared inadmissible as a policy rule is not justiciable and, therefore, a decision upon compensation for harm caused by a lawful policy rule is not justiciable either.

In the *Paul Krugerbrug* scenario, Liesbosch could thus invoke the policy rule before or after the permission was given. Should the Minister award no or too little compensation, Liesbosch could lodge an appeal and insist that the Minister award compensation in accordance with the *égalité devant les charges publiques* principle. Possibly, the Minister would have to decide on the compensation before granting the permission.

4.1.2. German law

Unlike in Dutch law, there is, in principle, only one possible legal basis in German law for the equalisation of the excessive impact that otherwise state action had upon a certain person. This basis is a parliamentary statute. If the legislator fails to provide such a basis and the state action proves to be individually excessive, the statutory basis of the state action will be unconstitutional and judges can set aside the state action.[52] The BVerfG also sets out certain requirements that the statutory basis has to fulfil. The legislator has to lay down the conditions for the claim to equalisation as well as the type and extent of equalisation.[53] If the statute meets the constitutional requirements, the competent administrative body has to decide upon equalisation when affecting property on the basis of the statute.[54] If it only awards compensation in money, the administrative body merely has to decide upon whether the holder of property rights has a claim to compensation, but not upon the amount.[55] The legislator has to include such obligations

49 ABRvS, Judgment of 12 November 2003, ECLI:NL:RVS:2003:AN7851, AB 2004, 95; ABRvS, Judgment of 8 November 2006, ECLI:NL:RVS:2006:AZ1762, AB 2007, 252; Van Buuren, in: T&C Algemene wet bestuursrecht, Article 3:4 Awb.

50 ABRvS, Judgment of 8 November 2006, ECLI:NL:RVS:2006:AZ1762, AB 2007, 252; Schueler 2002, p. 175.

51 ABRvS, Judgment of 16 April 2003, ECLI:NL:RVS:2003:AF7351, AB 2003, 347; see also: Van Ravels, NTB 2009, 42.

52 BVerfG, Decision of 2 March 1999, NJW 1999, 2877, 2879.

53 BVerfG, Decision of 2 March 1999, NJW 1999, 2877, 2879.

54 BVerfG, Decision of 2 March 1999, NJW 1999, 2877, 2879.

55 BVerfG, Decision of 2 March 1999, NJW 1999, 2877, 2879.

in the statute.[56] In the *Paul Krugerbrug* scenario, the statute that forms the basis for the plan to build the new non-moveable bridge would thus have to provide for an equalisation scheme. The planning authority would then have to decide upon equalising measures when adopting the plan. If it provides compensation in money, the planning authority only has to decide upon whether the holder of property rights has a claim to compensation. Should the statutory basis lack such a statutory basis or should the administrative body omit to take equalising measures, the affected holder of property rights has to appeal against the administrative decision. If the holder fails to do that, compensation can no longer be awarded.[57] *In casu*, if the bridge were located in the German State of Lower Saxony, Liesbosch could invoke §74(2), 2nd sentence, of the Administrative Procedure Act (VwVfG; *Verwaltungsverfahrensgesetz*), which is applicable according to §72(1) VwVfG, read in conjunction with §38(1), 1st sentence, of the Lower Saxonian Road Act (*Niedersächsisches Straßengesetz*). According to this provision, the competent administrative body has to oblige the project developer to take measures that are necessary to prevent a negative impact upon the rights of persons other than the entity that builds the bridge.

Liesbosch, however, could not bring an action for compensation on the basis of an expropriatory infringement (*enteignender Eingriff*). In cases where there was a statutory equalisation scheme, the BGH held that the expropriatory infringement would not apply.[58] If the statute lacked such a scheme, Liesbosch would have to appeal against the administrative decision, and the judge can set aside the state action. This is an expression of the priority of primary judicial protection (*Vorrang des Primärrechtsschutzes*).[59] Even the BGH acknowledges that no compensation can be awarded if the statutory basis of the state action does not provide for an equalisation scheme.[60] An action would only be successful if the legislator neither intended nor foresaw the excessive burden that state action imposed upon the holder of property rights on the basis of a statute.[61]

4.1.3. Comparative remarks

What is acknowledged under both German and Dutch law is that the state action with an individually excessive impact on property rights must be equalised. If necessary, judges have been taking equalisation measures on the basis of the principle of unusual sacrifice or *égalité devant les charges publiques* respectively. Whether these principles differ as to

56 BVerfG, Decision of 2 March 1999, NJW 1999, 2877, 2879.

57 BVerfG, Decision of 2 March 1999, NJW 1999, 2877, 2879.

58 BGH, Judgment of 30 June 1986, NVwZ 1987, 628, 628.

59 Ernst, in: MüKo-BGB, Vorbemerkung zu §903, No. 133.

60 BGH, Judgment of 5 May 1988, NJW 1989, 37, 39; BGH, Judgment of 10 December 1987, NJW 1988, 478, 480.

61 BVerwG, Judgment of 24 June 1993, NJW 1993, 2949, 2951; Von Arnauld 2002, p. 410; Ernst, in: MüKo-BGB, Vorbemerkung zu §903, No. 153 *et seq.*, with further references in fn 745. Some scholars conclude that there is no scope for the action on the basis of an expropriatory infringement: Wieland, in: Dreier, GG, Art. 14, No. 171; see for further references: Ernst, in: MüKo-BGB, Vorbemerkung zu §903, No. 152, fn 739.

the criteria for equalisation, is discussed in the third sub-section. However, what is a rather striking difference, is that German constitutional law, in principle, requires a statutory basis for equalisation measures, whereas under Dutch law compensation schemes can be based upon statute, a policy rule or an uncodified legal principle. Compared to the Dutch approach, the German approach has several advantages, but also various disadvantages. A statute enhances the democratic legitimacy of both the equalisation measures and the criteria to which they are subject. Not only does a statute have more formal democratic legitimacy than case law, it is also more likely to reflect the opinion of the people on whether it is just to equalise the consequences of a certain measure. Furthermore, it protects Parliament's budget authority.[62] If judges freely determine the criteria for equalisation measures, it may have a significant impact upon the State's budget.[63] Also, a statute provides more legal certainty than case law in that affected persons know beforehand that equalisation measures will be taken if certain criteria are met.[64]

The major disadvantage of such an approach is a lack of flexibility, which flexibility is the most important advantage of the Dutch approach. If there is no statute that provides for an equalisation scheme, the state action can be set aside as unlawful under German law if it turns out to be individually excessive. Liesbosch would have to lodge an appeal against the plan in order to obtain relief unless the BGH claims jurisdiction.[65] By contrast, Dutch law would put confidence in the judge's ability to find a just solution. The Dutch approach may therefore save infrastructure projects, such as the non-moveable Paul Kruger Bridge, from being blocked. Also, affected persons may find it more difficult to obtain judicial protection under German law. In principle, no equalisation measures will be taken unless the BGH claims jurisdiction. Instead, the BVerfG may first have to decide whether the state action is indeed individually excessive and an equalisation scheme had to be included in the statute. In such a case, the statute would be unconstitutional, and Liesbosch would have to wait in insecurity for the legislator to act.[66]

This does not mean, however, that the Dutch legislator sits back and does nothing. Title 4.5 of the Awb shows that the Netherlands have also moved towards the codification of the rules on compensation for individually excessive state action. Interestingly, Title 4.5 was enacted although there was no constitutional court that could threaten the legislator with the sanction of unconstitutionality of the whole statute affecting property.[67] Rather, a gradually growing public interest in a codification seems to have induced the

62 BVerfG, Decision of 2 March 1999, NJW 1999, 2877, 2879.

63 Cf. Tjepkema 2010, p. 28.

64 BVerfG, Decision of 2 March 1999, NJW 1999, 2877, 2879; Külpmann 2000, p. 219. See also: Draft of Title 4.5 of the Awb presented by the study group on compensation for lawful and unlawful state action, p. 9, available under: www.mkb.nl/download.php?itemID=476904 (last accessed: 28 August 2014).

65 Cf. Ernst, in: MüKo-BGB, Vorbemerkung zu §903, No. 154.

66 Külpmann 2000, p. 150 *et seq.*

67 Article 120 Gw stipulates that the judiciary cannot review the constitutionality of statutes.

Dutch government and Parliament to act.[68] By contrast, the German government was compelled to act by the BVerfG on the basis of the constitutional court's interpretation of the Basic Law. These findings suggest that German law and Dutch law subscribe to two different governance models with regard to constitutional matters, *in casu* the question what must be regulated by statute. To find out what the constitution requires, the Dutch system relies upon the self-control of Parliament and the responsiveness of the government and Parliament to the needs of society, whereas the German system rather entrusts the interpretation of the constitution to independent judges.

German law and Dutch law also follow different approaches when it comes to the moment at which the administrative body has to decide upon equalisation measures. Under German law, a unitary model applies because the administrative body has to decide upon equalisation measures when taking the decision on the substance. By contrast, Dutch law has adopted a mixed approach. In principle, the Dutch administrative body can choose whether it follows the unitary model in the form of the dependent decision on damages or the separation model, which means that it takes the independent decision on compensation in a separate trajectory after having taken the decision on the substance. The unitary model has some advantages. The affected person must decide whether or not to lodge an appeal against the state action. The BVerfG considered that it was not reasonable to expect this person to take this decision without knowing whether or not equalisation measures will be taken.[69] This approach would thus create more legal certainty for Liesbosch.[70] The advantage of the separation model is that the administrative body can further important projects, such as the non-moveable bridge in Utrecht, without having to worry that a court will strike down the decision because it has awarded no or insufficient compensation.[71]

4.2. *Forms of equalisation and compensation*

The German Basic Law not only subjects the basis of equalisation schemes to strict requirements, but also the form of equalisation. The BVerfG holds consistently that the legislator must ensure that the administrative body first takes measures that prevent harm to the property.[72] These measures include transitional arrangements, exemptions and other administrative or technological instruments.[73] This follows from the guarantee of existence (*Bestandsgarantie*) of property rights, entrenched in Article 14 GG. This guarantee of existence entails that Article 14 GG not only protects the value of the property right, but also its existence and its capacity to enhance the holder's freedom.[74]

68 Draft of Title 4.5 of the Awb presented by the study group on compensation for lawful and unlawful state action, p. 9 *et seq.*
69 BVerfG, Decision of 2 March 1999, NJW 1999, 2877, 2879.
70 Polak 2010.
71 Tjepkema 2010, p. 119.
72 BVerfG, Decision of 2 March 1999, NJW 1999, 2877, 2879.
73 BVerfG, Decision of 2 March 1999, NJW 1999, 2877, 2879.
74 BVerfG, Judgment of 17 December 2013, NVwZ 2014, 211, 214.

Only if such preventive measures prove to be unfeasible or disproportionately burdensome, can the legislator empower administrative bodies to award compensation in money.[75] Should the legislator fail to observe these rules, the statute will be unconstitutional, and Liesbosch must appeal against the state action so that judges will set it aside. Should the administrative body not take preventive measures according to those rules, Liesbosch also has to lodge an appeal against the state action. Liesbosch, however, may be able to circumvent this priority of preventive measures and claim compensation in money directly on the basis of an expropriatory infringement in cases where the BGH claims jurisdiction.[76]

In Dutch law, such a priority for preventing measures is neither institutionalised nor systematically observed. The rules on compensation based upon statutes, policy rules or case law, in principle, refer to compensation in money only.[77] The administrative authorities, however, are generally free to take preventive measures as well.[78] Provisions in some statutes, such as Article 6.1(1) of the Spatial Planning Act, stipulate that the administrative body will not award compensation if, and to the extent that, administrative measures prevent harm, but do not contain any obligation to take such measures.[79] Some policy rules entitle the administrative body to obtain advice on preventive measures.[80] Only some statutes provide for an obligation to take preventive measures before the administrative body takes the decision on the substance.[81] In practice, however, preventive measures play a bigger role, as judgments of the Judicial Division[82] indicate.

At first glance, there is no general obligation to take preventive measures first under Dutch law. As of yet, other legal instruments also fail to give priority to such measures. In particular, the proportionality test in terms of Article 3:4(2) Awb is not a suitable instrument to ensure it. As has been said above, unlike compensation in money, preventive measure can always be employed to reduce the weight of the disadvantages of an envisaged project and to make these disadvantages less likely to be disproportionate in relation to the goals of the project. One could therefore state that the proportionality test ensures the priority of preventive measures. However, this reasoning only applies as long as the disadvantages are disproportionate to the goals of the envisaged project. Once the disadvantages are no longer disproportionate to the goals, there is no obligation and, therefore, compelling incentive for the administrative body to take preventive

75 BVerfG, Decision of 2 March 1999, NJW 1999, 2877, 2879.
76 Ernst, in: MüKo-BGB, Vorbemerkung zu §903, No. 154.
77 De Graaf & Marseille 2014, No. 1055.
78 De Graaf & Marseille 2014, No. 1055.
79 ABRvS, Judgment of 27 April 2005, ECLI:NL:RVS:2005:AT4747, 2.6.
80 See, for instance, Article 16(2) Policy Rule on Compensation Infrastructure and Environmental Affairs 2014.
81 See, for instance, Article 10(1) lit. b of the Infrastructure Planning Act (*Tracéwet*).
82 See, for instance, ABRvS, Judgment of 9 July 2003, ECLI:NL:RVS:2003:AH9396, paras 2.5.3.2 and 2.6.2.4.

measures. Meanwhile, Liesbosch, the affected person in the *Paul Krugerbrug* case, may still bear an excessive burden, whereas the harm suffered by others may have been prevented or redeemed.

In this respect, German and Dutch law have thus adopted very diverse approaches. Whereas under the strict German approach administrative bodies are obliged to take preventive measures first, Dutch law, in principle, provides for compensation in money only and otherwise relies upon the abilities of Dutch administrative authorities to find more suitable measures to relieve the harm. From the perspective of German law, the Dutch approach violates the guarantee of existence of property rights because only the value of the property is protected. On the one hand, it gives administrative authorities an escape route for cases where preventive measures cause considerable, yet not disproportionate disadvantages.[83] On the other hand, affected holders of property rights, such as Liesbosch, may be inclined to allow harm to their property in exchange for money in order to use the funds for other purposes.[84] Should Liesbosch, however, wish to preserve their property as it is, Liesbosch will either have to engage in a dialogue with the competent Dutch authority or have to appeal against the decision on the substance and establish that Article 3:4(2) Awb has been violated. From a Dutch perspective, such an approach may cater for the necessary flexibility in practice, whereas the German approach may appear too focused on preserving a property right, even where affected persons do not wish to preserve it.

4.3. Criteria

This sub-section contains an analysis of the requirements to which Liesbosch's claim to equalisation is subject. Under Dutch law, Liesbosch could invoke the Policy Rule on Compensation Infrastructure and Environmental Affairs 2014. According to Article 2(1) of that policy rule, the Minister will award compensation to Liesbosch if the Minister or a representative of the Minister does harm to Liesbosch in the exercise of their powers and Liesbosch should not bear the harm. This claim to compensation is subject to several criteria, the two most important of which are the requirement of the individual burden (*speciale last*) and the requirement of the excessive burden (*abnormale last*). Art. 4 of the policy rule refers to the individual burden as harm that significantly differs from the harm done to others or as harm that is only done to a relatively small percentage of a group of people in the same position. In the Judicial Division's jurisprudence on compensation on the basis of the principle of *égalité devant les charges publiques*, an individual burden is referred to as harm that is done to a limited number of persons or entities.[85] What proves to be particularly difficult, is to determine the group in comparison to which Liesbosch is harmed more. There is no uniform application of this

83 Cf. ABRvS, Judgment of 9 July 2003, ECLI:NL:RVS:2003:AH9396, 2.6.2.4; Van Zundert, in: T&C Ruimtelijk bestuursrecht, Wet ruimtelijke ordening, Art. 6.1.

84 Cf. De Lange 1991, p. 168.

85 ABRvS, Judgment of 8 November 2006, ECLI:NL:RVS:2006:AZ1762, AB 2007/252.

criterion in the jurisprudence on infrastructure projects that affect an indefinite number of persons, but, as *Tjepkema* points out, there seems to be a tendency to rely exclusively on the criterion of the excessive burden.[86] The *Paul Krugerbrug II* judgment, the first judgment on this issue, may be viewed as the beginning of this development because the Judicial Division only refers the normal entrepreneurial risk. This forms part of the criterion of the excessive burden, as Article 3(1) of the policy rule shows. This provision defines the excessive burden as harm that is not a materialisation of the normal entrepreneurial or societal risk. This definition can also be traced in the Judicial Division's jurisprudence on compensation on the basis of the principle of *égalité devant les charges publiques*.[87] The factors that judges use to determine the normal entrepreneurial or societal risk are *inter alia* the foreseeability of the project and the amount of damage.[88] The importance of the project to the public good, however, does not play any role. As for Liesbosch's claim to compensation, it already follows from the Judicial Division's *Paul Krugerbrug II* judgment that the normal entrepreneurial risk does not entail the harm that Liesbosch suffers. Liesbosch could thus claim compensation on the basis of this policy rule.

In German constitutional law, the consequences of a definition of the scope and limits of property must be equalised where the state action imposes a disproportionate burden upon certain holders of property rights and where it imposes an unusual sacrifice that is contrary to the principle of equal treatment.[89] In such cases, the legislator will have to add an equalisation scheme to the statutory basis of the state action, *in casu* the statutory basis of the plan. What remains unclear, is the definition of the two alternative requirements for compensation, namely the disproportionate burden and the unusual sacrifice that is contrary to the principle of equal treatment. In the literature, many scholars assert that the courts should rely upon the extensive body of case law in the jurisprudence of the BGH on the action on the basis of an expropriatory infringement.[90] Compensation on the basis of an expropriatory infringement requires that an unusual sacrifice has been imposed upon the holder of property rights. Such an unusual sacrifice is defined as a particularly burdensome sacrifice for the public good upon certain persons or groups that it does not impose upon the other members of society.[91] On the basis of this criterion, the BGH developed normative thresholds for groups of cases.[92] Also, the BGH often seems to draw on from this body of jurisprudence without conducting a proportionality test.[93] By contrast, other authors insist that newly designed

86 Tjepkema 2010, p. 375.
87 ABRvS, Judgment of 8 November 2006, ECLI:NL:RVS:2006:AZ1762, AB 2007/252.
88 Tjepkema 2010, p. 429 *et seq.*
89 BVerfG, Decision of 15 September 2011, NVwZ 2012, 429, 430; BVerfG, Decision of 2 March 1999, NJW 1999, 2877, 2879.
90 Nolden 1997, p. 187; Cf. Ernst, in: MüKo-BGB, Vorbemerkung zu §903, No. 119, fn 609.
91 Külpmann 2000, p. 19.
92 Külpmann 2000, p. 27 *et seq.*
93 Kischel 2003, p. 608; Ernst, in: MüKo-BGB, Vorbemerkung zu §903, No. 119, fn 609.

proportionality tests and equal treatment tests must be conducted.[94] As to the proportionality test, it is submitted that these authors correctly conclude that the old jurisprudence of the BGH can no longer be used because the BVerfG requires a proportionality test instead of a particularly burdensome sacrifice. That means that the competent administrative body must balance the public interest in the non-moveable bridge against the disadvantages suffered by Liesbosch. The equal treatment test, however, does not need to be drafted from scratch as the BVerfG explicitly refers to the unusual sacrifice, which forms the core of the jurisprudence of the BGH. Following this reasoning, I conclude that Liesbosch would have a claim to equalisation because, as has been pointed out above, the plan to build the non-moveable bridge – at least – imposed an unusual sacrifice upon Liesbosch in terms of the jurisprudence of the BGH.

Irrespectively of this debate, Liesbosch could invoke §74(2), 2nd sentence, VwVfG. According to this provision, the competent administrative body has to oblige the project developer to take measures that are necessary to prevent a negative impact upon the rights of persons other than the entity that builds the bridge. Such measures are necessary if the negative effects caused by the project are unreasonable (*unzumutbar*).[95] The effects will be unreasonable if advantages of the project cannot justify its disadvantages.[96] In particular, the administrative body must scrutinise whether or not the negative impact is a common side-effect of the building of non-moveable bridges.[97] In the Paul Kruger Bridge scenario, it seems clear that the advantages of the non-moveable bridge cannot justify the loss of the viability of one's company, which cannot be considered a common side-effect of such a project. Liesbosch could thus demand that preventive measures be taken. All this does not apply if such measures are infeasible or incompatible with the project. Then, Liesbosch can claim appropriate compensation in money. §75(2), 2nd sentence, VwVfG concerns unforeseen consequences of the bridge and is therefore not applicable to Liesbosch.

This equalisation scheme complies with the constitutional requirements because it provides for equalisation measures for cases where a disproportionate burden is imposed upon a holder of property rights. As the BVerfG demands, only where preventive measures are infeasible or incompatible with the non-moveable bridge, will the administrative body be allowed to award compensation in money. It seemingly only concerns all cases where the non-moveable bridge imposes a disproportionate burden upon a holder of property rights. However, in the vision of the BGH, which still seems to apply, an unusual sacrifice that is contrary to the principle of equal treatment also requires a particularly burdensome effect on the holder of property rights. §74(2), 2nd sentence, VwVfG is thus likely to cover these cases as well.

94 Kischel 2003, p. 606 and 611; Rozek 1998, p. 237; Heinz & Schmitt 1992, p. 517 *et seq*; Ernst, in: MüKo-BGB, Vorbemerkung zu §903, No. 119.

95 Neumann, in: Stelkens/Bonk/Sachs, VwVfG, §74, Nos. 79 and 172.

96 Neumann, in: Stelkens/Bonk/Sachs, VwVfG, §74, No. 84.

97 Neumann, in: Stelkens/Bonk/Sachs, VwVfG, §74, No. 87.

A comparison of Dutch and German law shows that the claim to equalisation is subject to conditions. Not every state action must be equalised. Liesbosch, however, would be entitled to equalisation in either jurisdiction. The jurisdictions also use similar kinds of criteria, namely one criterion that measures the intensity of the impact upon the holder of property rights and one criterion that compares the impact of the project upon one holder to its impact upon others. Under Dutch law, these criteria are, in principle, cumulative; yet, there is a tendency in the field of infrastructure projects to rely upon the former criterion only. Under German law, in the unusual sacrifice test both criteria are applied as cumulative requirements, whereas the proportionality test serves to measure the intensity of the negative impact and balance these disadvantages against the public interest in the bridge. Moreover, the criterion that measures the intensity of the negative impact upon the holder of property rights may have different structures. Whereas the proportionality test under German law includes a balancing test, neither the unusual sacrifice test under German law nor the excessive burden test under Dutch law weigh the disadvantages against the advantages of the non-moveable bridge.

4.4. *Judicial protection*

In the previous sub-sections, I have made some observations about the judicial protection of Liesbosch. Not all of them are repeated here. This sub-section is confined to the extent to which judges review the decision to take preventive measures or to award compensation. It has been established that both Dutch and German law allow Liesbosch to appeal against the decision to take preventive measures or to award compensation in money. In Germany, the unitary model requires Liesbosch to appeal against the decision on the substance. In the Netherlands, Liesbosch either has to appeal against the decision on the substance or the independent decision on compensation, depending on the model that the administrative body applied. In Germany, the decision whether or not to take preventive measures according to §74(2), 2nd sentence, VwVfG is not of a discretionary nature, and there is no margin of appreciation.[98] That means that the decision is fully reviewed.[99] In the Netherlands, scholars widely consider the decision on compensation not to be of a discretionary nature.[100] Since 2003, the Judicial Division seems to agree.[101] However, *Tjepkema* asserts that there is a certain margin of appreciation as to the application of the excessive burden test and individual burden test, suggesting a limited review of that application.[102] On 5 December 2012, the Judicial Division confirmed that the criterion of normal entrepreneurial or societal risk grants

98 Neumann, in: Stelkens/Bonk/Sachs, VwVfG, §74, No. 177; BVerwG, Judgment of 11 November 1988, NVwZ 1989, 255, 256.

99 Schmidt-Aßmann, in: Maunz/Dürig, GG, Article 19(4), No. 181.

100 Tjepkema 2010, p. 424 *et seq*; De Graaf, Comment on ABRvS, Judgment of 15 December 2004, ECLI:NL:RVS:2004:AR7552, AB 2005, 67; Van den Broek 1999, p. 7.

101 ABRvS, Judgment of 14 July 2004, ECLI:NL:RVS:2004:AQ1051, AB 2005, 214; an example of a judgment of before 2003 that suggested that it was a discretionary decision: ABRvS, 14 November 2000, ECLI:NL:RVS:2000:AA8955, BR 2001, 234.

102 Tjepkema 2010, p. 424 *et seq.*

the administrative body a margin of appreciation.[103] In Germany, there is thus a full review of the application of all requirements for the claim to equalisation; in the Netherlands, it seems that the application of these requirements is only subject to limited review.

5. One last comparative remark

Although the consequences of the decision to build the bridge may have a quasi-expropriatory impact on Liesbosch, the decision does not constitute expropriation. This has a profound impact on the requirements for the legality of the decision. If the building of the bridge had required the acquisition of the property of Liesbosch, the expropriation of the property would have been subject to a proportionality test, *inter alia* a strict necessity test, under both Dutch and German law.[104] In particular, that means that the expropriation of the property and the extent to which it is expropriated would only be permissible if there were not any other equally suitable, but less invasive means to make possible the building of the bridge.

The State, however, does not expropriate or regulate Liesbosch's property, but merely physically affects it. That means that no separate expropriation procedure is followed, and that the administrative body does not need to conduct a proportionality test that exclusively concerns the infringement of Liesbosch's property. Instead, particularly when large infrastructure projects are planned, Liesbosch's property right is not the only property right that may be subject to legal or physical restrictions. Not affecting Liesbosch's property may lead to restrictions to someone else's and *vice versa*. This interdependence seems to result in a more lenient proportionality test. In German planning law, a specific project upon the holders of property rights will satisfy the necessity test if it is reasonably required to achieve the aim of the project's statutory basis.[105] The BVerwG holds consistently that a project would be reasonably required if it satisfied a need that is reflected by the goals of the applicable Act of Parliament.[106] *In casu*, the non-moveable bridge would enhance the local infrastructure and would thus contribute to the achievement of the goals of the Lower Saxonian Road Act. In the framework of the balancing of relevant interests, alternatives are scrutinised, and the affected interests, such as Liesbosch's, are weighed. The courts examine alternatives as to whether they are evidently better suited to achieve the aim of the project's statutory basis.[107] When the affected interests are weighed, the administrative body must find a

103 ABRvS, Judgment of 5 December 2012, ECLI:NL:RVS:2012:BY5105, para 7.2. Previously, the Judicial Division at least once subjected the application of those requirements to a full review. Judgment of 16 November 2005, ECLI:NL:RVS:2005:AU6237.

104 BVerfG, Judgment of 17 December 2013, NVwZ 2014, 211, 215; Den Drijver-van Rijckevorsel *et al.* 2013, p. 23 *et seq.*

105 BVerwG, Judgment of 9 November 2006, NVwZ 2007, 445, 447.

106 BVerwG, Judgment of 16 March 2006, NVwZ-Beil. 2006, 1, 15.

107 BVerwG, Judgment of 9 November 2006, NVwZ 2007, 445, 449 *et seq*; Söfker, in: Ernst *et al.*, BauGB, §1, No. 202.

balance between the public interest in the projects and adversely affected interests so that the disadvantages of the project are not disproportionate in relation to its contribution to the public good.[108] In particular, the administrative body must assess whether there is an equally suitable, but less invasive means to achieve the goal of the project's statutory basis.[109] This requirement is likely to prove toothless as alternative projects that affect one interest less often entail disadvantages for other interests.[110] In Dutch law, there is a similar phenomenon. The decision of the planning authority only does not satisfy the necessity test if the chosen alternative has considerable disadvantages compared to other alternatives.[111]

The conclusion would be that under Dutch and German law, the legal obstacles for an infrastructure project are considerably higher once the project requires the acquisition of the property. By contrast, if the State does not need to acquire it and merely regulates or physically affects the property, the legal protection of the property of Liesbosch as it is before the project is implemented is considerably weaker. This applies regardless of whether or not the state action has a quasi-expropriatory effect. In my opinion, it is very doubtful whether this difference in treatment is justifiable. Besides, the practical consequences of this phenomenon are likely to be greater in the Netherlands than in Germany. Unlike Dutch law, German law requires that the administrative body first take preventive measures before awarding compensation in money. The chances that the property will be preserved as it is are thus higher under German law.

6. Conclusion

German and Dutch law would both classify the plan to build the non-moveable bridge in Utrecht as individually excessive state action due to its physical impact on the property rights of Liesbosch. German and Dutch lawyers would also agree that not every state action with an impact on property rights must be equalised or compensated. Equalisation or compensation, however, is due if two criteria are met, namely one criterion that measures the intensity of the impact upon Liesbosch and one criterion that compares the impact of the project upon Liesbosch to its impact upon other holders of property rights. Furthermore, judges in both jurisdictions fully review equalising measures and awarded compensation.

The institutional arrangements and governance approaches in German and Dutch law, by contrast, differ significantly. In the German system, the legislator is constitutionally obliged to add an equalisation scheme to the statute that may foreseeably lead to individually excessive state action. Otherwise, the statute will be unconstitutional.

108 Söfker, in: Ernst *et al.*, BauGB, §1, No. 201.

109 Söfker, in: Ernst *et al.*, BauGB, §1, No. 201.

110 Van Zundert, in: T&C Ruimtelijk bestuursrecht, Wet ruimtelijke ordening, Article 6.1; De Lange 1991, p. 143.

111 ABRvS, Judgment of 3 August 2005, ECLI:NL:RVS:2005:AU0427; ABRvS, Judgment of 9 July 2003, ECLI:NL:RVS:2003:AH9396, 2.9.10.3; De Moor-van Vugt 1995, p. 230.

Compensation schemes in the Netherlands, by contrast, are to date primarily based upon case law and policy rules. In the future, Title 4.5 Awb, however, will provide a uniform statutory compensation scheme in the Netherlands. The role of the administrative body that took the restrictive decision is different. Whereas Dutch administrative bodies can in most cases choose whether to award compensation when they take the decision or to award compensation only later, German administrative bodies are obliged to take equalising measures when they take the decision.

Another difference lies in the type of measure equalising the individually excessive state action. Under German constitutional law, it follows from the guarantee of existence of property rights that proportionate and suitable measures that prevent the detrimental effects of the administrative decision have to be taken first. Dutch law, by contrast, only provides for an obligation to pay compensation in money. Other measures are optional, which may show that Dutch law only subscribes to a guarantee of value of property rights.

A similarity between German and Dutch law is that the state action with an individually excessive impact on property rights is treated as an orphan when compared to its big brother, expropriation. Under Dutch and German law, the forced transfer of property rights is subject to considerably stricter requirements than the individually excessive state action. However, as the individually excessive state action may have a severe impact on the use of the land and may threaten the economic viability of the holder of property rights, the mere fact that the holder retains their property rights does not seem a sufficient justification of these differences. Further research should therefore be done into differences between state action with an individually excessive impact on property rights and expropriation and the justification thereof.

Bibliography

Von Arnauld 2002
Von Arnauld, A., 'Enteignender und enteignungsgleicher Eingriff heute', *Verwaltungsarchiv* 2002, p. 394–417.

Bauschke & Kloepfer 1971
Bauschke, E. & Kloepfer, M., 'Enteignung, enteignungsgleicher Eingriff, Aufopferung', *Neue juristische Wochenschrift* 1971, p. 1233–1239.

Van den Broek 1999
Van den Broek, G.M., 'Nadeelcompensatieregelingen: bevoegdheid of verplichting?', *Bouwrecht* 1999, 1, p. 1–12.

***Contributor*, in: Dreier, GG**
Dreier, H. (ed.), *Grundgesetz, Kommentar*, Band I: Präambel, Art. 1–19, Commentary, 3rd ed., Tübingen: Mohr Siebeck, 2013.

Den Drijver-van Rijckevorsel *et al.* 2013
Den Drijver-van Rijckevorsel, J.E.F.M., Van Engen, A.W., Mulder, F.A. & Rus-van der Velde, M., *Handboek onteigening*, 4th ed., Deventer: Kluwer, 2013.

Elzinga, De Lange & Hoogers 2014
Elzinga, D.J., De Lange, R. & Hoogers, H.G., *Van der Pot, Handboek van het Nederlandse staatsrecht*, 16th ed., Deventer: Kluwer, 2014.

***Contributor*, in: Ernst *et al.*, BauGB**
Ernst, W., Zinkahn, W., Bielenberg, W. & Krautzberger, M. (eds.), *Baugesetzbuch*, Commentary, 114th ed., Beck: Munich, 2014.

De Graaf & Marseille 2014
De Graaf, K.J. & Marseille, A.T., *Nadeelcompensatie en onrechtmatige overheidsdaad*, The Hague: Boom, 2014. Reprinted from: Damen, L.J.A., Albers, C.L.G.F.H., Nicolaï, P., de Graaf, K.J., Jans, J.H., Klap, A.P., Marseille, A.T., Olivier, B.K., Vermeer, F.R., Klingenberg, A.M. & Tolsma, H.D., *Bestuursrecht, Deel 1*, 4th ed., Boom: The Hague, 2013.

Heinz & Schmitt 1992
Heinz, K. & Schmitt, K., 'Vorrang des Primärrechtsschutzes und ausgleichspflichtige Inhaltsbestimmung des Eigentums, Tendenzen und Wandlungen des Eigentumsschutzes auf Grund der neueren Rechtsprechung', *Neue Zeitschrift für Verwaltungsrecht* 1992, p. 513–522.

Hennekens 2000
Hennekens, H.P.J.A.M., 'Nadeelcompensatie: wanneer en waarom?', *Gemeentestem* 2000 (7130), 1, p. 569–575.

Kischel 2003
Kischel, U., 'Wann ist die Inhaltsbestimmung ausgleichspflichtig?', *Juristenzeitung* 2003, p. 604–613.

Külpmann 2000
Külpmann, C., *Enteignende Eingriffe?: das Entschädigungsinstitut des enteignenden Eingriffs und die neuere verfassungsrechtliche Dogmatik der Eigentumsgarantie*, Berlin: Duncker & Humboldt, 2000.

De Lange 1991
De Lange, R., *Publiekrechtelijke rechtsvinding*, Zwolle: W.E.J. Tjeenk Willink 1991.

***Contributor*, in: Maunz/Dürig, GG**
Herzog, R., Scholz, R., Herdegen, M. & Klein, H.H. (eds.), *Maunz/Dürig, Grundgesetz*, Munich: C.H. Beck.

De Moor-van Vugt 1995
De Moor-van Vugt, A.J.C., *Maten en gewichten, Het evenredigheidsbeginsel in Europees perspectief*, Zwolle: W.E.J. Tjeenk Willink, 1995.

***Contributor*, in: MüKo-BGB**
Gaier, R., Baldus, C., Commichau, M., Damrau, J., Eickmann, D., Engelhardt, H., Ernst, C., Füller, J.T., Joost, D., Heinemann, J., Kanzleiter, R., Kohler, J., Oechsler, J., Von Oefele, H., Pohlmann, P., Schmidt, K., Westermann, H.P. & Krone, F. (eds.), *Münchener Kommentar zum Bürgerlichen Gesetzbuch: BGB*, Band 6, Sachenrecht, §§854–1296, 6th ed., Munich: C.H. Beck, 2013.

Nolden 1997
Nolden, F., *Die ausgleichspflichtige Inhalts- und Schrankenbestimmung des Eigentums am Beispiel des Naturschutzrechts*, Kiel: Christian-Albrechts-Universität, 1997.

Polak 2010
Polak, J.E.M., 'Ontwikkelingen op het terrein van de overheidsaansprakelijkheid; over grenzen van privaatrecht en bestuursrecht heen', *Nederlands Tijdschrift voor Bestuursrecht*, 2010, 46, p. 315–323.

Van Ravels 2009
Van Ravels, B.P.M., 'M.H. Bregstein, de Hoge Raad en nadeelcompensatie', *Nederlands Tijdschrift voor Bestuursrecht*, 2009, 42, 320–324.

Riedel 2012
Riedel, D., *Eigentum, Enteignung und das Wohl der Allgemeinheit*, Berlin: Duncker & Humboldt, 2012.

Rozek 1998
Rozek, J., *Die Unterscheidung von Eigentumsbindung und Enteignung*, Tübingen: Mohr Siebeck, 1998.

Schlössels 2002
Schlössels, R.J.N., 'Nadeelcompensatie en het égalité-beginsel: chaos of ius commune? (I)', *Gemeentestem* 2002 (7160), 1, p. 149–159.

Schueler 2002
Schueler, B.J., 'Goede besluiten met slechte gevolgen. De verplichting tot nadeelcompensatie in het bestuursrecht', in: J.E. Hointink (ed.), VAR, Vereniging voor Bestuursrecht, *Schadevergoeding bij rechtmatige overheidsdaad*, VAR-reeks 128, The Hague: Boom, 2002, p. 91–199.

***Contributor*, in: Stelkens/Bonk/Sachs-VwVfG**
Stelkens, P., Bonk, H.J. & Sachs, M. (eds.), *VwVfG: Verwaltungsverfahrensgesetz*, 8th ed., Munich: C.H. Beck, 2014.

***Contributor*, in: T&C Algemene wet bestuursrecht**
Borman, T.C., Van Buuren, P.J.J., Jacobs, M.J. & De Poorter, J.C.A. (eds.), *Tekst & Commentaar Algemene wet bestuursrecht*, 8th ed., Deventer: Kluwer, 2014.

***Contributor*, in: T&C Ruimtelijk bestuursrecht**
Van Zundert, J.W., Fortgens, A.C., De Haan, P.M.J. & Nijmeijer, A.G.A. (eds.), *Tekst & Commentaar Ruimtelijk bestuursrecht*, 7th ed., Deventer: Kluwer, 2014.

Tjepkema 2010
Tjepkema, M.K.G., *Nadeelcompensatie op basis van het égalitébeginsel*, Deventer: Kluwer, 2010.

Van Zundert 1980
Van Zundert, J.W., *Overheidsbestuur en grondeigendom*, Alphen aan den Rijn: Samson, 1980.

Rafael Ibarra Garza*

THE REAPPEARANCE OF OWNERSHIP AS A MEANS OF SECURITY IN MEXICAN AND FRENCH LAW, THE BATTLES BETWEEN LEGAL TECHNIQUE AND LEGAL POLICY IN INSOLVENCY LAW

1. Introduction

In Mexican and French law, the right of ownership is at the heart of several legal techniques that secure the performance of an obligation. The retention of title clause, the lease purchase agreement and the trust are examples of such techniques. The use of ownership as a means of security is nothing new; it was used in Roman law.

With the abolition of the *nexum* or debt bondage, the person of the debtor could not be used as collateral anymore.[1] Therefore, the Romans created a trust like device, named *fiducia cum creditore*, to secure the payment of a debt. The settlor would transfer ownership to the trustee as collateral to secure the performance of an obligation; where the trustee would be the creditor and the settlor, the debtor.[2] Subsequently, if the settlor breached the contract, the trustee could sell the trust property and pay himself with the price paid.[3] On the other hand, if the settlor performed his obligation the trustee returned the trust property.[4]

In time this mechanism disappeared,[5] giving way to new security devices, such as the *pignus* (pledge) and the *hypotecha* (mortgage).[6] These techniques did not use ownership as a means of security in Roman law, nor do they in Mexican and French law. Even

* Universidad Autónoma de Nuevo León (Facultad de Ciencias Políticas y Administración Pública); Leal-Isla & Horváth, S.C. Email: ribarra@lealisla.com.mx, ribagar@hotmail.com.
I thank Carlos Ibarra for language editing.

1 Gaudemet 2000, p. 18.

2 Geny 1885, p. 63ff.

3 Barrière 2004, para. 21.

4 Gaudemet 2000, p. 300.

5 Authors have found various reasons of the disappearance of the *fiducia cum creditore*. One explanation is the lack of adequate protection of the beneficiaries' interests (Cantin-Cumyin 1992, para. 12; Lajarte 2009, para. 10). Another explanation is the disappearance of the formalities *mancipatio* and *in iure cession* (Jordano Barea 1959, p. 558).

6 Gaudemet 2000, p. 269.

though the pledge and the mortgage continue to exist in Mexican and French law, the use of the right of ownership as collateral not only has reappeared; it has been successful. This is quite astonishing because the pledge and the mortgage are more sophisticated mechanisms.

Even if we know that the refinement of a legal system does not prevent the revival of ancient techniques and therefore that the law has 'cyclical movements: institutions are born, eclipse and reappear',[7] we cannot avoid enquiring upon these reappearances because at first instance it seems unreasonable. Thus, we can ask ourselves the following question: if the right of ownership ceased to be used to secure the performance of an obligation under Roman law, why has it reappeared in Mexican and French contemporary law?

Answering this question will be the cornerstone of this paper. The question will be answered by confronting legal technique and legal policy in the realm of securities and insolvency. However, before we continue with the inquiry we must shed some light on legal technique and legal policy.

By legal technique we simply refer to the legal mechanisms and rules that apply to them; in other words, we denote how those legal mechanisms function in a particular legal system.[8] Therefore, when we mention, for example, the legal technique of the right of ownership we simply refer to the manner in which that right legally functions. As to legal policy, in this paper it is intended to be understood as the government objectives that underlie legal rules.[9] For example, the main objective of Mexican and French insolvency law is to preserve business; consequently many insolvency rules are drafted in pursuit of that objective.

The comparative method will be used to answer the question stated above. Specifically, we will compare Mexican and French law. The reason for undertaking a comparative study is that it permits us to leave our legal way of thinking and therefore detect non-perceived realities of our legal system.[10] In other words, by the comparative method we will be able to see our law through a new light; as Marcel Proust once wrote '[t]he real voyage of discovery consists, not in seeking new landscapes, but in having new eyes'.

7 Perrot 1953, para. 47.

8 For general literature on technique, see Demogue 2001, p. 200–237; Perrot 1953. For literature on legal technique, see Geny 1921, para. 179–186; Perrot 1953, para. 5–11; Dabin 1935, p. 1–102.
Nevertheless, we must keep in mind that each legal mechanism has internal rules which are specific to each mechanism and it has external rules which are not specific to the mechanism but affects it anyway. For example, the rules of insolvency law are not specific to the mortgage but have an effect on that mechanism.
Therefore it is possible to analyse the way in which a specific mechanism functions intrinsically; without the effects of external legal rules. We can also analyse how that same specific mechanism functions globally by taking into account external rules.

9 For literature on legal policy, see Cossío Díaz 2010, p. 170–184.

10 Legrand 2009, p. 209; Muir Watt 2000, para.18.

As we will see, the reappearance of ownership as collateral is the outcome of two battles: the battle between the legal technique of traditional real securities, on the one hand, and, on the other hand, the legal policy of insolvency law and the battle between the legal technique of the right of ownership, on the one hand, and the legal policy of insolvency law on the other hand.

2. The legal technique of traditional real securities versus the legal policy of insolvency law

When the performance of an obligation has been postponed to a future date, the creditor is at risk of default by the debtor. Time is always a factor of risk because between the creation of an obligation and its performance, the economic situation of the debtor can change for the worse;[11] during this time not only can the debtors' assets be lost, they can also lose value and his liabilities may increase. Therefore, the creditor may find himself upon an insolvent debtor.

This places the creditor in a perilous situation because, even though Article 2964 of the Mexican Civil Code and Article 2284 of the French Civil Code provide that the debtor is liable for the performance of its obligations with all his assets (present and future), if the debtor has insufficient assets to meet all his liabilities, the principle of equality among creditors applies. This means that the value of the assets will be distributed proportionately between all the creditors;[12]thus, they will only be partially paid.[13]

The effects created by the proportional distribution of the debtors' assets between the creditors led to the creation of legal techniques that secure the performance of an obligation.[14]Among the various legal techniques that secure the performance of an obligation, we find those that can be classified in Spanish as *garantías reales* and in French as *sûretés réelles* (in English both they could be translated as 'real security').[15]

In Mexican and French law a real security is a right created over assets to secure the performance of an obligation.[16]Among the different types of real securities we have the

11 Villegas 1988, p. 7.

12 Article 222 of the *Ley de Concursos Mercantiles* (Mexican Bankruptcy Act).
For French authors on the principle of equality among creditors, see Bougerol-Prud'Homme 2010, para. 89; Pérochon 2012, para. 3.

13 So for example if there are three creditors one for 120 euros, a second for 80 euros and a third for 50 euros the total debt amounts to 250 euros. Now if the debtors' assets are valued at 100 euros, this means that he may only pay 40 per cent of the total debt. Therefore, each creditor will be paid 40 per cent of his debt which in our case the first creditor will be paid 48 euros, the second will be paid 32 euros and the third only 20 euros.

14 Bourassin, Brémond & Jobard-Bachellier 2012, para. 4.

15 See Smith 2013, p. 307.

16 As opposed to *garantías personales/sûretés personnelles* (Spanish/French) where the performance of an obligation is secured by another party assuming responsibility for the obligation of a debtor if the debtor defaults.

pledge and the mortgage. One of the main features of these traditional guarantees is that they confer on the creditor a priority; the creditor, holder of a real security (in our case the pledgee and the mortgagee), has the right to be paid, from the proceeds of the sale of the secured asset, before other creditors.[17] Therefore, by the use of the pledge and the mortgage, the creditor avoids the inconveniences caused by the principle of equality among creditors; so if the asset "given" as security is worth at least as much as the debt, the creditor will be fully paid.

If an atomistic approach corroborates that the pledge and the mortgage confers a priority, a holistic approach exposes limitations on that priority; as the French proverb states "*toute médaille a son revers*". In other words, if we step out of the realm of real securities and take into consideration insolvency rules, the pledgee and the mortgagee will encounter another landscape.

As we will see, the opening of bankruptcy proceedings against the owner of the asset which serves as security (generally the debtor himself), will not only paralyze the execution of the pledge and the mortgage, but also the priority conferred by those securities may also be lost. Because of these limitations, the pledge and the mortgage become inefficient and cause economic insecurity to the pledgee and the mortgagee.

The limitations imposed on the priority of the pledgee and the mortgagee seem irrational. The reason why real securities were created was to avoid the inconveniences of an insolvent debtor. Hence, it is mind-boggling that the pledge and the mortgage become inefficient upon the insolvency of the debtor, which is when the creditor needs them the most. Given that credit is so important to our economy and efficient real securities are important as they provide access to more and cheaper credit,[18] the limitations mentioned above also seem unreasonable from an economic perspective.

For these reasons we must ask ourselves about the legal reasoning behind the limitations imposed by insolvency law on the priority of the pledgee and mortgagee. To understand those limitations we will start by studying the development of French insolvency law and the legal policies which underlie that body of law.[19]

The traditional solution upon the debtors' insolvency was to end the debtors' business by organizing the liquidation of his assets and distribute the proceeds of the sale among creditors.[20] This demonstrates that the legal policy of insolvency law was the protection of the creditors' interests. Although the liquidation of the debtors' assets continues to be

17 For the Mexican mortgage, see Article 2893 of the Civil Code; for the Mexican pledge, see Article 2856 of the Civil Code; for the French mortgage, see Article 2323 of the Civil Code; for the French pledge, see Article 2333 of the Civil Code.

18 Bourassin, Brémond & Jobard-Bachellier 2012, para. 3.

19 We will only take into consideration the reforms that are directly linked to our subject matter.

20 Pérochon 2012, para.1–5.

part of bankruptcy proceedings, the protection of the creditors' interests ceased to be the primary legal policy of French insolvency law.

The first reform that had an impact on pledgees and mortgagees was the law no. 67–563 of 13 July 1967. Since this reform, creditors with real securities have to prove their rights before they could enforce their guarantees; therefore the rights to enforce their guarantees are suspended until their rights were proved in the bankruptcy proceedings. Prior to this law, creditors were not subject to any restrictions, and this is why one author states that secured creditors begin to resemble unsecured creditors.[21]

If the reform of 1967 curtailed the rights of secured creditors, it was not until the law no. 85–98 of 25 January 1985 that the situation of pledges and mortgages was turned upside down. The new purpose of bankruptcy proceedings was to "protect the company, continue operations, conserve employment and settle liabilities".[22] Therefore, the new law had two hierarchized objectives; the first objective was to preserve business while the second objective was the payment of creditors.[23] In other words, the new legal policy of French insolvency law was to avoid the liquidation of the company.

The change of legal policy is comprehensible because companies produce goods and services and offer employment; therefore, they are institutions of grave social and economic importance.[24] When a company is liquidated there will be one less taxpayer, there will be one less producer, there will be unemployment and it may have a domino effect causing other bankruptcies.[25] For this reason, French legislators consider that the survival of insolvent companies is in the interest of the general public and for that reason worthy of protection.[26]

The priority to preserve business is not unique to French law; the second paragraph of the first article of Mexico's Commercial Insolvency Law establishes that "it is in the public interest to preserve businesses and prevent a generalized default of obligations which threatens their viability and that of other businesses with which it has a commercial relationship".[27]

Given that the preservation of business is the main legal policy in both Mexican and French insolvency law, in both countries the payment of creditors is subordinated to the

21 Pérochon 2012, para. 10.

22 "*sauvegarde de l'entreprise, le maintien de l'activité et de l'emploi et l'apurement du passif*" (Article 1 of the law of 25 January 1985).

23 Pérochon 2012, para. 12.

24 Pérochon 2012, para. 1.

25 Pérochon 2012, para. 1.

26 Pérochon 2012, para. 1.

27 "*Es de interés público conservar las empresas y evitar que el incumplimiento generalizado de las obligaciones de pago ponga en riesgo la viabilidad de las mismas y de las demás con las que mantenga una relación de negocios*" (Translation made by the author).

preservation of the company. Consequently, in our case, the right of the pledgee and the mortgagee to enforce their securities is paralysed.[28] This is so because, if it were possible to enforce the creditors' rights during bankruptcy proceedings, the assets of the debtor would be diminished and subsequently it may become impossible for the company to continue its operations.[29]

The preservation of business is not the only legal policy that undermines the pledge and the mortgage. In both Mexican and French insolvency law, protection is given to certain group of creditors (for example, the employees of the debtor).[30] The protection is conferred by establishing priority in payment; this means that certain group of creditors will paid before others.

Unfortunately, in both countries the pledgee and mortgagee are not highly ranked; this means that they will not be paid until those better ranked creditors are. However, if privileged creditors deplete the debtors' assets before payment can be made to the pledgee and mortgagee, the debtor will not have sufficient assets and the pledgee and mortgagee will never be paid.

Accordingly Mexican and French bankruptcy proceedings place two limitations on the pledgee and the mortgagee: on the one hand, the enforcement of security interests is suspended and, on the other hand, the preferential right of the creditor is subordinated to the payment of other privileged creditors. It is obvious that the legal policy of bankruptcy law was triumphant in the battle against the legal technique of traditional real securities; having as an outcome the inefficiency of these securities when the creditor needs them the most: upon the bankruptcy of his debtor.

Once traditional real securities had become inefficient and failed to protect creditors, legal practitioners had to create new techniques to protect their clients.[31] They saw in the right of ownership a possible escape from the policies of bankruptcy law. Therefore, the final outcome of this battle was the reappearance of the right of ownership as collateral in Mexican and French law. However, for the legal technique of ownership as a means of security to survive it must overcome the legal policies of bankruptcy law.

3. The legal technique of the right of ownership versus the legal policy of bankruptcy law

As seen above, because of the legal policies of Mexican and French insolvency law, traditional securities became inefficient and failed to protect creditors; therefore, legal

28 Article 65 of the Mexican Bankruptcy Act (*Ley de Concursos Mercantiles*).

29 In this sense, see case [TA]; 9ª Época; TCC; SJF y su Gaceta; Tomo XI, Enero de 2000; p. 1006.

30 For Mexican law, see Article 217 ff. of the Bankruptcy Code (*Ley de Concursos Mercantiles*); for French law, see Pérochon 2012, para. 808 ff. and 1126 ff.

31 In this sense, see Bougerol-Prud'Homme 2010, para. 8.

practitioners had to use or create other techniques to protect their clients. More precisely, it was necessary to find a legal technique that could protect the creditor upon the insolvency of the debtor.

Legal practitioners turned to the right of ownership as a possible escape from the policies of insolvency law. Theoretically, if ownership is retained by,[32] acquired by[33] or transferred to the creditor[34] as collateral, then those assets are not owned by the debtor and therefore cannot be part of his bankrupt estate. Consequently, the creditor may avoid bankruptcy proceedings and the other creditors of his debtor, just by claiming ownership. Technically, this is how the creditor would enforce his security and how the right of ownership as collateral should function both in Mexican and French law.

However, the efficiency of the right of ownership as collateral is not guaranteed because its enforcement is contrary to the legal policies of both Mexican and French insolvency law. First of all, the legal technique of ownership as a means of security is contrary to the legal policy of preservation of business; the effect of this policy is the suspension of the enforcement of any obligation. This suspension should include the creditors' right to claim ownership when this right is used as a security device.[35] On the contrary if creditors with ownership rights as collateral are to be permitted to claim their ownership, the debtor will be left with fewer assets to continue its activities and so his financial viability will deteriorate; having as a final possible effect the liquidation of the company and therefore contrary to the main objective of insolvency law of both countries.

In addition to the policy stated above, both Mexican and French insolvency law protect the interests of certain creditors by conferring them priority in payment over others.[36] Hence, the creditors' with a right of ownership as security should in principle not be permitted to claim ownership until the preferential creditors have been paid. Consequently, if creditors are allowed to claim ownership before preferential creditors are paid, their interests which insolvency law pretends to protect will be curtailed. As a

32 An example would be the retention of title clause in a sales contract (for Mexican law, see Galindo Garfias 1978, pp. 82–85; for French law, see Voinot 2014). In Mexican and French law ownership of the sold goods is transferred *solo consensus*; which means that ownership is transferred from the seller to the buyer immediately when the contract is concluded. Therefore, if the seller supplies the sold goods on credit, he may secure payment by retaining title of those goods until the buyer fulfills his obligations.

33 An example would be the lease purchase agreement (for Mexican law, see Rodríguez Elorduy 1991, pp. 149–154; for French law, see Aynès & Crocq 2013, para. 806–808), where a creditor, instead of loaning money to the debtor to acquire a specific property, buys property himself then leases it to the debtor with an option for the latter to buy it. Therefore, the creditor by acquiring property has secured payment.

34 An example would be the trust as a means of security (for Mexican law, see Suayfeta Ozaeta 2003, pp. 85–106; for French law, see Simler & Delebecque 2012, para. 677–683), where a creditor asks the debtor to transfer property to him (or to a third party) as security, and the creditor (or the third party) holds that property as trustee until payment of the debtor.

35 See section 2 of this paper.

36 See section 2 of this paper.

result, permitting the legal technique of ownership as collateral to function as it technically should, would be contrary to another legal policy of insolvency law of both countries.

From the above, it is obvious that a conflict exists between the legal technique of the right of ownership as security and the legal policies of Mexican and French insolvency law. Therefore, in the scenario that the debtor becomes insolvent, the efficiency of the right of ownership as collateral cannot be guaranteed; it is possible that in both countries the right of ownership will surrender to the legal policies stated above. The history of French law demonstrates this possibility; before the law named Dubanchet, of 12 May 1980, the retention of title clause (a type of security based on the right of ownership) was ineffective in bankruptcy proceedings.[37]

If the right of ownership as collateral reappeared as a solution to the perilous situation of creditors upon the insolvency of their debtors,[38] it will not survive unless it overcomes the battle that is fought with the legal policies of insolvency law. Therefore, we must analyse the efficiency of the right of ownership in Mexican and French positive law.

In Mexico the conflict described above firstly finds a solution in a general rule, which later is confirmed by various specific rules. The general rule is found in Article 70 of the Mexican Bankruptcy Act (*Ley de Concursos Mercantiles*); this article establishes that if the assets held by the debtor are identifiable, and if the right of ownership has not been irrevocably transferred to the debtor, the assets may be separated by their rightful owners. If the assets which are in the hands of the debtor remain identifiable, then the creditor would be able to claim ownership because no right of ownership has been transferred to the debtor; on the contrary ownership was acquired by, retained by or transferred to the creditor. Thus, in accordance with this general rule the legal technique of the right of ownership overcomes the legal policies of Mexican insolvency law.

However, as specific rules prevail over general rules,[39] the efficiency of the right of ownership as collateral will therefore depend on there being no special rule that contradicts the general rule stated above. The Mexican Bankruptcy Act (*Ley de Concursos Mercantiles*) specifically provides that property leased to the debtor can be claimed by the lessor[40] and that trust property in the hands of the debtor can be claimed by the trustee.[41] Thus, when the creditor has used the lease purchase agreement or a trust to secure payment, then ownership may be claimed by the righteous owner which in our case is the lessor and the trustee. In contrast to the lease purchase agreement and the

37 On the retention of title clause and its introduction to bankruptcy proceedings, see Houin 1980.
38 See chapter 2.
39 This is so because special rules reveal a clearer intent of the lawmaker than general rules.
40 Article 71, VII, a).
41 Article 71, VII, e).

trust, nothing is said about the retention of title clause, thus we can conclude that the general rule applies or that the special rules stated apply by analogy.

Consequently, a bankruptcy proceeding in Mexico does not affect creditors which have secured the performance of an obligation with a right of ownership; the proceedings do not suspend the creditors' right to enforce his security, nor do they subordinate the enforcement of the security to the payment of preferential creditors. If the creditor wants to enforce his security, and therefore claim property, he will have to return the debtor the price that was paid for the asset and perform any obligation that derived from the asset object of the security.[42]

French law is a lot more complicated than Mexican law because French insolvency is more sophisticated; each mechanism has its own set of rules. The rules that apply to the retention of title clause are different from those that apply to the trust, which are also different from those that apply to the lease purchase agreement. However, as we will see, despite the different rules that apply to each mechanism, the legal technique of the right of ownership as collateral also overcomes the legal policies of French insolvency law; and they are, therefore, an efficient means of security.

Regarding the retention of title clause, Article L. 624–9 of the French Commercial Code provides that the creditor may claim ownership. The only condition is that the creditor must claim ownership within three months upon the commencement of the bankruptcy proceedings.[43]

If the creditor preferred to secure payment by the use of a trust, different rules apply to different scenarios: either the trustee maintains the possession of the trust property or the possession rests in the hands of the debtor. When the trustee maintains possession, although bankruptcy proceedings have been opened against the debtor, this has no effect on the trust property and therefore the trustee can execute the security.[44] However, when the debtor has possession of the trust property, Article L. 622–23–1 of the French Commercial Code provides that the possession of trust property cannot be transferred to the trustee or a third party; therefore the right of the trustee to claim ownership is paralyzed by the bankruptcy proceedings.[45] The trust is considered by French Insolvency Law as a *contrat en cours* which means it will continue despite the bankruptcy proceedings.[46] Nevertheless, once the liquidation procedure starts, the trust as a security device recuperates its efficiency; trustee may claim ownership and therefore leap over the preferential rights of preferential creditors.[47]

42 Article 73 of the Mexican Bankruptcy Act (*Ley de ConcursosMercantiles*).
43 On this subject, see Bougerol-Prud'Homme 2010, para. 509 ff.
44 See Article L. 622 VI of the French Commercial Code; see Bougerol-Prud'Homme 2010, para. 513.
45 In this sense, see Bougerol-Prud'Homme 2010, para. 512.
46 See Article L. 622–13 of the French Commercial Code.
47 See Article L. 642–7 para. 5; see Bougerol-Prud'Homme 2010, para. 512.

When the creditor has secured payment through a lease purchase agreement, there are two possible scenarios. Either the regime of *contrat en cours* applies to the lease purchase agreement or it does not and the agreement will be terminated upon or during bankruptcy proceeding. If the agreement is considered as a *contrat en cours*, the performance of the lease will be continued despite bankruptcy proceedings of the lessee-debtor; consequently, the lessor-creditor may not claim ownership of the leased asset; nonetheless, the lessor-creditor is well protected because the instalments due since the bankruptcy proceedings will continue to be paid and the lessee-debtor still has the option to acquire the leased asset.[48] Conversely, if the lease purchase agreement is terminated upon or during bankruptcy proceeding, the lessor-creditor may claim ownership of the leased asset and therefore avoid or get out of the bankruptcy proceeding of his debtor and thus not compete with preferential creditors.[49] Therefore, in both scenarios the lease purchase agreement secures payment even when the debtor becomes insolvent.

4. Conclusion

When Mexican and French legislators subordinated the pledge and the mortgage (traditional real securities) to the legal policies of preservation of business and the protection of preferential creditors of insolvency law, the efficiency of these securities was curtailed and left creditors unprotected upon bankruptcy proceedings of their debtors. This economic insecurity obliged creditors to find or create new mechanisms to secure payment; they turned to the right of ownership as a means of security. Once the right of ownership reappeared in both Mexican and French law it became a successful security device because it overcame the same legal policies of insolvency law which caused the inefficiency of traditional securities. Therefore, by the use of the right of ownership the creditor efficiently secured payment in spite of the insolvency of the debtor.

In other words, the reappearance of the right of ownership as collateral in Mexican and French law is explained by the different battles fought between legal technique and legal policy in the realm of insolvency law. While the triumph of the legal policies of insolvency law over the legal technique of traditional securities is the reason of the reappearance of ownership as a security device, the triumph of the legal technique of ownership right over the legal policies of insolvency law explain the endurance of the right of ownership as collateral in both Mexican and French law.

48 Bougerol-Prud'Homme 2010, para. 515.

49 Article L. 624-10-1 of the French Commercial Code; Bougerol-Prud'Homme 2010, para. 515.

Bibliography

Aynès & Crocq 2013
Aynés, L. & Crocq, P., *Les Sûretés, La Publicité Foncière*, Paris: LGDJ, 2011.

Barrière 2004
Barrière, F., *La réception du trust au travers de la fiducie*, Paris: Litec, 2004.

Bougerol-Prud'Homme 2010
Bougerol-Prud'Homme, L., 'Exclusivité et garanties de paiement', Thesis Paris, 2010.

Bourassin, Brémond & Jobard-Bachellier 2012
Bourassin, M., Brémond, V. & Jobard-Bachellier, M.-N., *Droit des sûretés*, Paris: Sirey, 2012.

Cantin-Cumyin 1992
Cantin-Cumyin, M., 'Avant-Projet de la Loi Relatif à la Fiducie, du Point de Vue Civiliste d'Outre-Atlantique', *D.* 1992, p. 117 ff.

Cossío Díaz 2010
Cossío Díaz, J. R., *Derecho y Análisis Económico*, México: FCE, ITAM, 2010.

Dabin 1935
Dabin, J., *La technique de l'élaboration du droit positif, spécialement du droit privé*, Paris: Recueil Sirey, 1935.

Demogue 2001
Demogue, R., *Les notions fondamentales du droit privé. Essai critique*, Paris: La Mémoire du Droit, 2001.

Galindo Garfias 1978
Galindo Garfias, I., 'La transmisión de la propiedad entre vivos', in: J.A. Sánchez Dávila (ed.), *Libro del Cincuentenario del Código Civil*, Ciudad de México: UNAM, 1978, p. 71 ff.

Gaudemet 2000
Gaudemet, J., *Droit privé romain*, Paris: Montchrestien, 2000.

Geny 1885
Geny, F., 'Étude sur la fiducie', Thesis Nancy, 1885.

Geny 1921
Geny, F., *Science et technique en droit privé positif, vol. III*, Paris: Recueil Sirey, 1921.

Houin 1980
Houin, R., 'L'introduction de la clause de réserve de propriété dans le droit français de la faillite', *D.* 1980, Chr. p. 293.

Jordano Barea 1959
Jordano Barea, J. B., *El Negocio Fiduciario*, Barcelona: Bosch, 1959.

Lajarte 2000
Lajarte, C., 'La nature juridique des droits du bénéficiaire d'un contrat de fiducie', *Rev. Lamy dr. civ.*, 2009, p. 71 ff.

Legrand 2009
Legrand, P., 'La comparaison des droits expliquée à mes étudiants', in: P. Legrand (ed.), *Comparer les droits, Résolument*, Paris: PUF, 2009, p. 209 ff.

Muir Watt 2000
Muir Watt, H., 'La fonction subversive du droit comparé', *RID comp.* 2000, p. 503ff.

Pérochon 2012
Pérochon, F., *Entreprises en difficulté*, Paris: LGDJ, 2012.

Perrot 1953
Perrot, R., *De l'influence de la technique sur le but des institutions juridiques*, Paris: Recueil Sirey, 1953.

Rodríguez Elorduy 1991
Rodríguez Elorduy, A., 'El Arrendamiento Financiero en México', *Rev. Admon. Púb.* 1991, no. 81, pp. 149–154.

Simler & Delebecque 2012
Simler, Ph. & Delebecque, Ph., *Droit Civil, Les Sûretés, La Publicité Foncière*, Paris: Dalloz, 2012.

Smith 2013
Smith, L., 'Security', in: A. Burrows (ed.), *Oxford Principles of English Law, English Private Law*, Oxford: Oxford University Press, 2013.

Suayfeta Ozaeta 2003
Suayfeta Ozaeta, J., 'La Institución Jurídica del Fideicomiso en Caída Libre. En Proceso Nuevas Reformas a las Leyes que lo Regulan', *Rev. Der. Priv.* 2003, no. 6, pp. 85–106.

Villegas 1988
Villegas, C. G., *El Crédito Bancario*, Buenos Aires: Depalma, 1988.

Voinot 2014
Voinot, D., 'Réserve de Propriété', *Rép. Com.* 2014.

List of Abbreviations

Chr.	Chronique
D.	Recueil Dalloz
ed.	Editor
ff.	Following pages
ITAM	Instituto Tecnológico Autónomo de México
LGDJ	Librairie Générale de Droit et de Jurisprudence
n°	Number
p.	Page
para.	Paragraph
pp.	Pages
PUF	Presses Universitaires de France
Rép. Com.	Répertoire de Droit Commercial
Rev Lamy dr civ	Revue Lamy du Droit Civil
Rev. Admon. Púb.	Revista de Administración Pública
Rev. Der. Priv.	Revista de Derecho Privado
RID comp	Revue International de Droit Comparé
SJF	Semanario Judicial de la Federación
TA	Tesis Aislada
TCC	Tribunales Colegiados de Circuito
UNAM	Universidad Nacional Autónoma de México

Johan Van de Voorde*

ON THE UNITY OR DISUNITY OF ACQUISITIVE AND EXTINCTIVE PRESCRIPTION. OR HOW DARING REINTERPRETATIONS ARE NOT ALWAYS RIGHT

1. Introduction

1. Research question. The *Code Napoléon* seems to treat the acquisitive and the extinctive prescription as a unity. They are both treated in the same title (Book III, Title XX *Prescription*). They share the same noun, only modified by an adjective. Many rules, especially those on the running of time (suspension, interruption, calculation), are common. And both consolidate facts that have existed during a certain time without being disputed.[1] Does this mean that the prescription is a unity, that there is no real difference between acquisitive and extinctive prescription?

To study this question, we will start with a short explanation of the majority theory, which posits the disunity (dualism) of both types of prescription. Then we will analyse some arguments in favour of the unity (monism) of the two types of prescription, and finish with an analysis of these arguments.

2. Relevance. Why is the unity or disunity of prescription of any interest? Traditionally, extinctive prescription obeys other rules than acquisitive prescription. Extinctive prescription is considered to require only the inaction of the creditor, while acquisitive prescription requires possession. If the two types of prescription are a unity, then extinctive prescription would also require possession. That possession will need to be qualified, without vices (i.e. without qualities that render it suspicious and thus 'unworthy' of having legal effects): it has to be "*une possession continue et non interrompue, paisible, publique, non équivoque, et à titre de propriétaire*", a possession which is "continuous, peaceable, public, unambiguous and as owner" or in other words *nec vi, nec*

* University of Antwerp, Research Group Personal Rights and Property Rights.
1 Wintgen 2010, p. 385.

clam, nec precario (Article 2229 C.Nap.).[2] In a unitary (or monist) theory of prescription, it would become more difficult to extinguish a debt by prescription.

3. Studied countries. This contribution takes Belgian law as its starting point. As Belgian civil law is, in its origins, mainly French,[3] French law is also studied. Next to these, Dutch, German and English law are studied too, but only in a subsidiary way.

2. Majority theory

4. Majority theory: disunity (duality) of the two types of prescription. A clear majority of Belgian (and French) academics considers acquisitive and extinctive prescription to be essentially different in their application, effects and mechanism. Extinctive prescription extinguishes a right[4] solely because of the running of time[5] and concerns both personal and real rights.[6] Acquisitive prescription implies the original acquisition of a right,[7] necessitates a qualified possession during a certain time[8] and only concerns real rights.[9] Only acquisitive prescription has retroactive effect,[10] extinctive prescription does not.[11] That is the theory. Practically, the differences are less pronounced as both types of prescription need the passing of a certain time, calculated in the same manner.

Let us now analyse whether this majority position is correct.

3. Is the majority right?

5. Emerging doubts. In an notorious article, F. Zenati and S. Fournier argue for the unity of prescription.[12] In their opinion, all extinctive prescriptions are actually disguised acquisitive prescriptions. They consider that the debtor is to possess his debt during a sufficiently long time, after which he acquires his debt. Then he is his own creditor. A debt cannot exist when its debtor and its creditor are the same person, so that it is then extinguished by 'consolidation' (cfr. Article 1300 C.Nap.).

2 In this contribution, for reasons of simplicity only the acquisitive prescription of a property right is considered.
3 On the influence of French law on Belgium, see Bouabdallah 2014.
4 Willems 2011, p. 194–199, nos. 239–245; De Page and Dekkers 1953, p. 74, no. 86.
5 Laurent 1878, p. 6, no. 1; De Page and Dekkers 1953, p. 73, no. 86; Lecocq 2012, p. 169, no. 55.
6 Lecocq 2012, p. 170, no. 55; Laurent 1878, p. 18, no. 8; De Page and Dekkers 1953, p. 73, no. 86.
7 De Page and Dekkers 1953, p. 74, no. 86; Lecocq 2012, p. 169, no. 55. But there are some who say that the acquisitive prescription leads to the *transfer* of an existing real right, not a creation of a new one: Mignot 2009, no. 52 (descriptive).
8 Lecocq 2012, p. 169, no. 55; De Page and Dekkers 1953, p. 73, no. 86.
9 De Page and Dekkers 1953, p. 73, no. 86; Lecocq 2012, p. 169–170, no. 55. Because, at least in Belgian, French and Dutch law, personal rights could also be the object of real rights (one can be the 'owner' or usufructuary of a claim), personal rights are indirectly concerned as well.
10 De Page and Dekkers 1957, p. 1147–1148, no. 1281.
11 *France:* Mignot 2009, no. 15.
12 Zenati and Fournier 1996, p. 344 e.v.

6. Plan. This contribution will first study the legislative context in which the Code Napoléon was written. Then, the text of the Code Napoléon and of other civil codes will be studied to ascertain whether they support a monist or dualist conception of prescription. Hereafter, the concept of 'negative possession' (possession of a debt by the debtor) will be studied, as this is an essential requirement for the monist conception of prescription.

3.1. Historical arguments: the legislative context of the Code Napoléon

7. Monist legislative tendencies. The 'ancient law' (law as it was before the French Revolution) has several monist tendencies concerning prescription.[13] The Parisian customary law (as reformed in 1580) is a good example. Its Article 114 treats the extinctive prescription of real rights, especially rents[14] and hypothecs.[15] To acquire this prescription, the debtor has to be in possession during a certain time and in good faith. The terms used are functionally identical to those of Article 113, which regulates the shortened acquisitive prescription of immovable property.[16] At least some commentaries treat these articles as one, even though Article 114 regulates extinctive prescription and Article 113 regulates acquisitive prescription.[17]

8. Domat. Domat, known for his influence on the codifiers of the Code Napoléon, sounded remarkably monist when he wrote that "*la possession est une maniere d'acquerir & de perdre le droit de propriété d'une chose, & tout autre droit, par l'effet du tems.*"[18] Nevertheless, a fuller lecture indicates that he was not monist, as he also wrote that no possession was needed for the prescription of rights and actions (*droits et actions*).[19] Strangely, Zenati and Fournier do not give much attention to this, only observing that Domat considers the prescription of incorporeal rights as both extinctive and acquisitive.[20]

9. Pothier. Pothier, another important influence on the Code Napoléon, was unabashedly against the unity of the two types of prescription. In the beginning of his *Traité de la prescription*, he writes that "*La prescription dont nous traitons ici, n'a rien de commun, que le nom, avec celle qui a fait la matière du huitième chapitre de la troisième partie de notre Traité des Obligations.*"[21] Remarkably, he considers "*l'affranchissement des rentes, hypothèques et autres charges réelles*" (the type of prescription of Article 114 of the Parisian customary law) to be an acquisitive prescription.[22] Nowadays, the type of

13 Zenati and Fournier 1996, p. 341–342.

14 In present day law, rents are no longer real rights. The law of the Ancien Régime considered the *rentes foncières* to be real rights.

15 Although the article only named rents and hypothecs, all limited real rights were considered to fall in its ambit: Pothier 1825, p. 451, no. 136; Martin 1972 p. 94.

16 See also Martin 1972 p. 86, 94.

17 Charondas le Caron 1605, p. 86.

18 Domat 1756, p. 272–274 (book III, title VII, section IV, no. I and *passim*). Spelling as in the original.

19 Domat 1756, p. 275 (book III, title VII, section IV, no. X).

20 Zenati and Fournier 1996, p. 342.

21 Pothier 1825, p. 389, no. 1.

22 Pothier 1825, p. 389, no. 1, 451, no. 136.

prescription which leads to the loss of real rights because of non-use, is considered to be an extinctive prescription.[23] This makes clear that Pothier is more complex than it would seem.

10. Negative possession. The 'negative possession' – the possession of a debt by the debtor by not paying it and not being ordered to pay by the creditor – is an important element of the monist view of prescription. It also appears occasionally in the ancient law. D'Argentré uses it twice in his commentary on the Breton customary law.[24] Only the second example is interesting for this article. It concerns the "*moulins banaux*" (mills which the inhabitants of a place were obligated to use because of feudal law). The feudal lord can build a banal mill and force the people of his vassals to use this mill. But if a vassal were to build his own banal mill, he could demand 'his' people back. The lord could not use acquisitive prescription to defend himself from this demand, but there was an exception. If the vassal had demanded his people back and the lord had formally refused and stayed in possession for another 40 years, he would have acquired the right to keep those people.

11. Dualist tendencies. The monist tendencies which we have shown, are but one side of the coin. For Duplessis, the customary law of Maine contained a dualist type of prescription.[25] His *Traité des prescriptions* was therefore divided in two parts, the first on acquisitive prescription, the other on extinctive prescription.[26]

12. Conclusion. There is a certain support for a monist view of prescription in the ancient law. Most notable is the position of the French customary law, which makes no difference between acquisitive and extinctive prescription. Several important authors also write in a monist way. Nevertheless, that support is often ambiguous (e.g. Domat does not consider possession necessary for extinctive prescription, though his definition of prescription is monist) and there are countercurrents which support the dualist view of prescription.

3.2. *Textual arguments: the words of the legislator*

3.2.1. The Code Napoléon

13. Strong tendencies towards monism. The *Code Napoléon* shows a number of strong monist tendencies. The most obvious is Article 2229, which says that "*pour pouvoir prescrire, il faut une possession continue et non interrompue, paisible, publique, non équivoque, et à titre de propriétaire.*"[27] No difference is made between acquisitive and

[23] Sagaert 2012–2013, p. 1474, no. 5.

[24] Hevin, d'Argentré and Du Moulin 1746, p. 105 and 715.

[25] Duplessis 1728, p. 217.

[26] Duplessis 1728, p. 218.

[27] The Dutch translation of art. 2229 BW suggests that only the acquisitive prescription falls within the ambit of this article: "*Om iets door verjaring te verkrijgen, is vereist een voortdurend en onafgebroken, ongestoord, openbaar, niet dubbelzinnig bezit, als eigenaar.*" Nonetheless, the French text is better to ascertain the will and words of the legislator.

extinctive prescription. Neither is there any general article that expressly excludes extinctive prescription by limiting the requirement of possession to acquisitive prescription.

Article 2222 C.Nap. forbids the renunciation of an acquisition by prescription by those who are not capable of transferring a right. This suggests that the renunciation of an acquisition by prescription is actually a retrocession of a right.[28]

Article 2226 C.Nap. makes it impossible to acquire a right by prescription when this right is *extra commercium*. This article is also used to declare actions other than real rights which are *extra commercium* (e.g. actions concerning legal descent of persons) incapable of prescribing, even though their prescription (if admitted by law) would be extinctive.[29]

And finally, Article 2219 C.Nap. defines prescription as a means to acquire something or to be liberated of an obligation. In conjunction with Article 712 C.Nap. (according to which prescription is a means to acquire property), this suggests that the liberation is technically attained because the debtor acquires his debt. This means that the debtor becomes his own creditor, so that the debt is extinguished by a process sometimes called 'confusion' or 'consolidation'.[30] Some authors have also read Articles 2219 and 2262 C.Nap. in conjunction to deduct that the extinctive prescription of a limited real right transfers that right back to the proprietor.[31]

14. Structural monism. Title XX *Prescription* of book III of the Code Napoléon is divided into five chapters: general provisions, possession, causes which render prescription impossible, causes of interruption or suspension and finally the time needed for prescription. Nowhere is there a structural difference between acquisitive and extinctive prescription. On the contrary: the chapter on possession is treated on the same footing as the other (generally applicable) chapters, even though this does not make sense in a dualist system of prescription.

15. Dualist elements. However interesting the tendencies towards monism may be, the Code Napoléon also contains elements favourable to a dualist theory of prescription. Articles 617 and 705–706 name both extinctive prescription and consolidation as ways for usufruct and servitudes to end. As the extinctive prescription actually works by consolidation – at least in the monist interpretation of prescription –, this is either indicative of a dualist type of prescription or of a lack of knowledge of the manner in which extinctive prescription functions.

28 Zenati and Fournier 1996, p. 351.

29 Zenati and Fournier 1996, p. 351.

30 See art. 617 C.Nap. for an example: usufruct ends "*Par la consolidation ou la réunion sur la même tête, des deux qualités d'usufruitier et de propriétaire*" ("By the consolidation or vesting in the same person of the two capacities of usufructuary and of owner").

31 Seresia 1873, p. 390–391, no. 261.

Another important argument for dualism is Article 2219 C.Nap.: if extinctive prescription were actually the same as acquisitive prescription, the legislator would not have said that prescription is a means to acquire a right *or* to be liberated of an obligation.[32]

16. Legislative intent. What did the legislators themselves have to say, outside of the words of the law? Not much, though Bigot-Préameneu is clearly dualist in his report to the *Corps législatif*: "*Par la prescription une chose est acquise lorsqu'on l'a possédée pendant le temps déterminé par la loi. Les obligations s'éteignent par la prescription, lorsque ceux envers qui elles ont été contractées ont négligé, pendant le temps que la loi a fixé, d'exercer leurs droits.*"[33] His words nevertheless cannot be decisive, as Portalis was the reporter in the *Conseil d'État* (but the discussion there was terse).[34]

17. Conclusion. It is obvious that the Code Napoléon lends much support to the monist theory of prescription, but at the same time there are also elements which show doubt. The Code Napoléon can therefore be considered ambiguous on this point.

3.2.2. Reform in France

18. Reform of 2008. In 2008 the French Parliament reformed a large part of the Code Napoléon, including the rules on prescription.[35] Strikingly, all elements which indicated a monist conception of prescription have been eliminated. Both forms of prescription are now treated in different titles (titles XX and XXI of book III). Article 2219 (new) C.Nap. expressly defines extinctive prescription as a loss of a right because of the inaction of the creditor. Only acquisitive prescription still needs possession (Article 2258 (new) C.Nap.).

3.2.3. Other Codes

19. Germany (BGB). The BGB differentiates both types of prescription clearly. Acquisitive prescription is regulated in §§937–945 (moveables) and 900 (immoveables) BGB. Extinctive prescription is treated in §§194–218 BGB. The running of time is regulated in the part on extinctive prescription, but a number of those provisions are declared applicable to acquisitive prescription as well. The objects of the two types of prescription are also different. §194 BGB declares that extinctive prescription concerns the *Anspruch*, while §937 BGB implies that acquisitive prescription concerns property rights. §199 BGB excludes possession as a condition for extinctive prescription, as the mere inaction of the creditor suffices. The provisions on acquisitive prescription all explicitly necessitate possession. Clearly, the BGB is a proponent of strict dualism.

32 Hansenne 1983, p. 31.

33 Fenet 1836, p. 573, 577.

34 Fenet 1836, p. 549.

35 This reform was enacted by law no. 2008-561 of 17 June 2008 *portant réforme de la prescription en matière civile.*

20. Netherlands (BW). Article 3:99 BW suggests a monist definition of prescription in Dutch law. It says in general terms that rights on goods are acquired by "uninterrupted possession" ("*onafgebroken bezit*"). Article 3:101 BW adds to that by saying that prescription starts running on the day after acquisition of possession. More expressly, the title above Articles 3:99–106 BW declares that these articles deal with the "acquisition and *loss* of goods." Goods are, in the words of Article 3:6 BW, all things and all patrimonial rights ("*alle zaken en alle vermogensrechten*") so that claims (*schuldvorderingen*) are goods. It is, therefore, imaginable that extinctive prescription operates indeed by acquisition by the debtor.

Article 3:309 BW might seem contrary to this analysis, but it could easily be interpreted as merely changing the time needed; nowhere is there any explicit exclusion of possession. The apparent need for possession is reinforced by Articles 3:309–310 BW. They make a number of cases of extinctive prescription dependent on the knowledge by the claimant of all relevant elements of the claim. When a claimant has full knowledge of his claim, but does not act, he can be considered to leave possession of the claim to the debtor.

However suggestive the laws are, the legislative intent was otherwise. The Dutch legislator desired to make a clear difference between acquisitive and extinctive prescription. He even said that the joint treatment of both types of prescription in the old Civil Code had been an error.[36] Originally, the title of Articles 3:99–106 BW was more clearly dualist: "acquisition by prescription" ("*verkrijging door verjaring*"). It was only Article 3.4.3.8a (presently Article 3:106 BW) that changed this, as this article extinguishes limited real rights when the action to guard them from infractions (the *action negatoria*) is prescribed.[37] The 'seat' of extinctive prescription is, following the intent of the legislator, Article 3:306 BW.[38]

The Dutch Civil Code contains a number of indications which favour a monist theory of prescription, but these are merely accidental. The legislator intended to make a firm difference between both types of prescription.

Conclusion. In a number of cases, the laws have some tendencies to the monist theory of prescription, but these are either accidental, or sufficiently counterweighted by dualist theories.

36 Van Zeben, Du Pon and Olthof 1981, p. 917.
37 Van Zeben, Du Pon and Olthof 1981, p. 408.
38 Van Zeben, Du Pon and Olthof 1981, p. 917.

3.3. *Common condition: the negative possession (possession of the debt by the debtor) in present-day law?*

3.3.1. Negative possession and the Code Napoléon

3.3.1.1. Continued life after 1804

21. Merlin and the *possession négative*. The Napoleonic *procureur-général* of the Court of Cassation, Ph.-A. Merlin de Douai, tended towards a monist theory of prescription.[39] In his *Répertoire universel et raisonné de jurisprudence* he treated prescription mostly as a conceptual unit, although there are also counterindications. He writes that acquisitive prescription is based on a presumption of transfer (because the owner has the right to possess, one has to presume that the possessor is owner) and subsequently considers the same reasons to underlie extinctive prescription.[40] But he then excludes possession from the list of requirements for extinctive prescription,[41] only to say something else later on: "*Pour écarter [la prescription libératoire] à l'aide de la maxime dont il s'agit, le défendeur n'a besoin que d'une possession négative, c'est-à-dire, de l'inaction de son adversaire, du défaut de poursuites ou d'exercice du droit de celui-ci. [...] [Le débiteur] a acquis, par la silence de son prétendu créancier, la possession de ne rien lui devoir [...].*"[42] The context indicates that Merlin sought an explanation for the exception of nullity which survives the prescription of the action in nullity (cfr. *quae temporalia sunt ad agendum, perpetua sunt ad excipiendum*), but this kind of prescription is a special case of extinctive prescription. There is no objection to using the same reasoning on extinctive prescription in general. But then, why not speak of it while treating extinctive prescription in general? Interestingly, several authors follow Merlin's lead and use negative possession to explain how an exception could survive the prescription of the claim.[43] It must be noted that Zenati and Fournier do not touch upon the exclusion of possession as a requirement for extinctive prescription.[44]

A more clearly monist definition of prescription can be found by G. de Chabrol-Chaméane, who wrote that "*La possession est la cause générale de la prescription.*"[45] Acquisitive prescription is foremost in his thoughts, but extinctive prescription is also discussed on a number of occasions. Nevertheless, nothing is said about the *possession negative*.

39 Zenati and Fournier 1996, p. 342–343.

40 Merlin de Douai 1827, p. 66–67.

41 Merlin de Douai 1827, p. 124.

42 Merlin de Douai 1827, p. 247.

43 Le Roux de Bretagne 1869, p. 205, no. 1114; Deffaux 1841, *v° prescription*, 228–229, no. 102; de Fréminville 1848, p. 325; de Fréminville 1845, p. 344, no. 903; Dalloz 1832, *v° prescription*, 403; Vazeille 1834, p. 244, no. 568.

44 Zenati and Fournier 1996, p. 342–343.

45 de Chabrol-Chaméane 1835, *v° prescription*, 374.

22. Fall of negative possession. The theory of negative possession did not survive long. Already in 1824 Vazeille wrote that extinctive prescription only needed the running of time, contrasting this with acquisitive prescription which also needed possession.[46] Around the middle of the 19th century, the work of Aubry and Rau assured the predominance of the dualist theory of prescription.[47] This effected the 'fall' of negative possession as explanation for the survival of exceptions.

23. Modern survival? Although the idea of negative possession seems to have disappeared, there still are some traces of it. The Napoleonic law of servitudes illustrates this. Servitudes can be extinguished by non-use (extinctive prescription) (Article 708 C.Nap.). A partial non-use is possible, at least if the non-use is due to a material obstacle such as a wall which blocks part of a servitude of way. Merely factual non-use is not sufficient for partial extinction of a servitude.[48] The owner of a dominant tenement who uses his servitude of way only to drive cars between a public road and his tenement (although he has wider rights which include the right to drive lorries) cannot later be forbidden to use his servitude also for lorries merely because in the last 30 years he has never done so.

The owner of the servient tenement can be considered to have a negative possession of the servitude, at least to the extent that the material obstacle is caused by him or should be eliminated by him.[49] The Breton customary law supports this analysis, as at least one author considered building higher than allowed by a servitude *non altius tollendi* to be a negative possession, sufficient for extinctive prescription.[50]

The full extinguishment of continuous servitudes is regulated in an analogous manner. Article 707 C.Nap. stipulates that the time for extinctive prescription of continuous servitudes only starts running when something is done which is contrary to the servitude (e.g. blocking the canal which irrigates the dominant tenement). This clearly suggests that the owner of the servient tenement has a negative possession of the servitude. Nonetheless, the act in breach of the servitude could come from a third party or from a chance event.[51] This makes it rather difficult to ascertain that the owner of the servient tenement has the needed *animus* and *corpus possidendi*.

3.3.1.2. Is negative possession acceptable?

24. Introduction. Zenati and Fournier have been severely criticized for positing (negative) possession as a requirement for extinctive prescription.[52] An important

46 Vazeille 1824, p. 23, nos. 26–27. See also the Belgian edition: Vazeille 1834, p. 10–11, nos. 26–27.

47 Aubry and Rau 1842, p. 181–182, §209; Zenati and Fournier 1996, p. 343.

48 Cass. 6 January 2006, no. C.04.0358.F. Sagaert 2012–2013, p. 1474, no. 5.

49 In other cases, art. 703 C.Nap. is to be applied so that no prescription is needed, unless it is to prevent art. 704 C.Nap. from having effect.

50 Poullain du Parc 1769, p. 248.

51 Sagaert 2014, p. 528, no. 658.

52 Lecocq 2003, p. 430, no. 4; Dross 2013, no. 10; De Page and Dekkers 1957, p. 835, no. 923.

problem is that negative possession implies the non-use of a right. The legal definition of possession (Article 2228 C.Nap.) stresses the exercise of a right, which is a positive action. Zenati and Fournier try to salvage their theory by saying that the possession is proven less by actions than by "*le rayonnement social.*"[53] They actually say that it is the 'view of the general public' ('verkeersopvattingen') which defines when a certain person is possessor. In Dutch law, this is a correct understanding of possession (Article 3:108 BW), but the Code Napoléon defines possession in a more objective way (Article 2228 C.Nap.). He who exercises power over a right is possessor because he exercises that power, not because he is considered to be the possessor. Nevertheless, in practice Dutch and Belgian law resemble each other more than one would infer from the black letter of the law,[54] without becoming identical.[55]

25. Problems with detention (houderschap, détention, Fremdbesitz). M.E. Storme writes that the possession of claims is necessarily mediated by the debtor: "*het goed wordt steeds gehouden via de schuldenaar, de prestatie ligt in diens handen.*"[56] In other words, a person possesses a claim because the debtor considers him to be the creditor. This makes that the debtor is detentor of the debt. Article 2236 C.Nap. however forbids the detentor to acquire the thing he holds by way of prescription, unless there has been an interversion of title (i.e. an act which transforms the detention in possession: the detentor who buys the thing he holds, thereby becomes possessor). But this problem is not insurmountable, as Article 2241 C.Nap. stipulates that one can prescribe against one's title (e.g. detentorship) if this prescription would liberate one from a debt or limited real right.

There might be a more important problem. Generally, the detentor is obliged to give back the goods which the owner has entrusted to him. Article 2236 C.Nap. implies that the detentor (and his heirs) continues to be a detentor, even when his obligation to give back the goods is extinguished by prescription. The owner could therefore ask his goods back with a *rei vindicatio.* In the monist theory, one would not expect the *rei vindicatio* to be viable. At least, the detentorship should disappear once the title of detention has disappeared: how can the detentor continue to be a detentor if the obligation of restitution which made him a detentor obliges him to give the goods to himself? Contrary to this, the dualist theory can explain why the detentor continues to be a detentor. A part of the title of detention survives the extinctive prescription.[57]

53 Zenati and Fournier 1996, p. 345–346, vn. 21.

54 Vuye 2003, p. 327 et seq.

55 In Belgian law, the absence of the *animus possessionis* excludes possession (see e.g. Ghent 4 January 2002, *AJT*, 2001–02, 874, *RW*, 2004–2005, 144). In Dutch law, it is quite thinkable that a person without *animus possessionis* would be considered possessor: Bartels, van Mierlo and Ploeger 2013, p. 104, no. 118.

56 Storme 2000, p. 332; Rutten 2011, p. 106–107, no. 113.

57 See about the most important theories on the effects of extinctive prescription: Willems 2011, p. 193–199, nos. 238–245. See also §194 BGB, which restricts the effect of the German extinctive prescription to the *Anspruch*.

26. Problems with interversion of title. As we already explained, a detentor can make himself a possessor by way of interversion of title. This is an act by which the detentor denies the right of the possessor (in such a way that he knows of it) and claims that right for himself.[58] Some authors state that such an interversion also has to occur before a negative possession is possible.[59] This may provoke practical problems, as merely refusing or omitting to pay a debt (such as rent to a lessor) is not sufficient for an interversion of title: the refusal must be accompanied by a pretence that one is the owner.[60] This problem can be solved with Article 2241 C.Nap. (prescription to liberate oneself from an obligation is possible against a 'title'), but it still is a bad mark for the monist theory. In the dualist theory, Article 2241 C.Nap. merely clarifies a point which was already clear from the fact that there is an extinctive prescription. In the monist theory, Article 2241 C.Nap. is essential to make the prescription of claims possible without too many practical problems.

27. Contra non valentem... For Zenati and Fournier, the suspension of a case of prescription effected by the adage *contra non valentem agere, non currit praescriptio* (against him who is not capable to act, the prescription does not run) is actually a vice of possession, to wit, its ambiguity.[61] In their theory, extinctive prescription is explained as a presumed transfer of the claim to the debtor. If the creditor cannot act (he does not know about the claim, is forced to abstain from claiming because he is in prison, is in coma, ...) then any presumption of a transfer is laughable.

In French law, this is an interesting thought. Belgian law, though, does not accept the adage *contra non valentem...*, even if there are some scant countervoices.[62] Article 2251 C.Nap., as interpreted in Belgium, restricts the causes of suspension of prescription to those admitted by law.[63] Only for legal impediments is there an exception.[64] Mere

58 Laurent 1878, p. 334, no. 323; De Weggheleire 2013, p. 903, no. 4; Vuye 1994, p. 55–56, no. 48; De Page and Dekkers 1952, p. 748, no. 850; Rutten 2011, p. 527.
France: Jourdain 1995, p. 31, no. 30; Baudry-Lacantinerie and Tissier 1924, p. 262, no. 333; Lecocq 2012, p. 133, no. 29.

59 See e.g. Hevin, d'Argentré and Du Moulin 1746, p. 715.

60 De Page and Dekkers 1952, p. 748, no. 850.

61 Zenati and Fournier 1996, p. 347.

62 See e.g.: Court of Appeal of Liège 4 january 1993, *JLMB*, 1994, 558. Lecocq 2012, p. 194, no. 63 (nuanced); Dekkers and Dirix 2005, p. 520, no. 1244, 523, no. 1255 (nuanced); Hansenne 1983, p. 85, no. 133; Verjans 2014, p. 161–162, no. 32. See also Art. 31 KB 18 maart 1935 no. 150 tot samenschakeling van de wetten betreffende de inrichting en de werking van de Deposito- en Consignatiekas en tot aanbrenging van wijzigingen daarin krachtens de wet van 31 juli 1934, *BS*, 21 maart 1935, 1.778. Vranckx, Coremans and Dujardin, p. 21; *RPDB*, I, v° *Caisse des dépots et consignations*, 801, no. 38.

63 Court of Appeal of Brussels 16 january 2002, *Res jur.imm.*, 2002, 95. De Page and Dekkers 1957, p. 1108–1109, no. 1237; Van Oevelen 1987, p. 1821, no. 58; Van Oevelen 2000–2001, p. 1444, no. 24; Van Drooghenbroeck and Marchandise 2010, p. 470, no. 67; Masschelein 2010, p. 197–198, no. 283.

64 Van Oevelen 1987, p. 1821, no. 58; Lecocq 2012, p. 194, no. 63; Hansenne 1983, p. 85, no. 133; Van Drooghenbroeck and Marchandise 2010, p. 471, no. 69; Van Oevelen 2000–2001, p. 1444, no. 24; Dekkers and Dirix 2005, p. 524, no. 1255; Verjans 2014, p. 160, no. 28.

force majeure or even inescapable legal errors do not, on the contrary, suspend prescription.[65]

28. Vices of possession? If there is a negative possession, there can also be vices of possession. The monist theory indeed explains better the adage *contra non valentem* as a vice of (negative) possession – at least if that adage is accepted, which it is not in Belgian law. But are the other vices of possession so practically viable? If a debtor is poor or his assets are difficult to get at, a creditor may abstain from exercising his claim as he would lose more by acting than by abstaining.[66] If, on the other hand, a debtor is very rich and powerful, a creditor may abstain because his debtor would be able to mount a substantial legal defence. Is the lack of any exercise of a claim a result of a tacit transfer or is it an unhappy result of special circumstances? These cases, which are relatively frequent, all seem to suffer from ambiguity, which is a vice of possession. Extinctive prescription would often be impossible in this system. This would render it unable to promote legal security, although this is a major justification for prescription. Zenati and Fournier do not examine this, so their position is unclear.

29. *Animus possidendi*? Does the debtor have a sufficient *animus possidendi*? One may accept this when the debtor knowledgeably refuses to pay or abstains from paying. *A fortiori* when the debtor loudly and clearly refuses to pay, or openly takes possession.[67] But what if the debtor does not pay because of an error, or because the invoice never reached him? Bank accounts are another problem area. Many bank accounts can be debited on first demand: the bank has to pay when and only when the customer orders it. It is difficult to say that a bank possesses the funds in an account when it is ready and willing to execute the transactions ordered by the customer – at least if such orders were given.

30. *Corpus possidendi*? There are also some problems concerning the *corpus possidendi* when using the monist theory of prescription. An example may be the best way to illustrate this. Aulus Agerius gives a lifelong usufruct on a piece of land to Numerius Negidius, who pays him fully for this transfer. Numerius Negidius exercises his rights personally during about 20 years, but then he falls gravely ill. Because of his illness he forgets about his usufruct so that no one actually uses the piece of land. Aulus Agerius has no knowledge of the illness of Numerius Negidius and has better things to do than to go and look at some faraway piece of land. He therefore exercises no power over his piece of land. As Numerius Negidius already has paid the full price of the usufruct, there is nothing which alerts Aulus Agerius. How could Aulus Agerius then be said to have taken possession of the usufruct? Even if Numerius Negidius has lost his possession (but loss of possession is relatively difficult), that does not mean that Aulus Agerius has taken

[65] Van Drooghenbroeck and Marchandise 2010, p. 471, no. 68; Verjans 2014, p. 159, no. 28; Van Oevelen 2000–2001, p. 1444, no. 24; De Page and Dekkers 1957, p. 1109–1112, no. 1238; Van Oevelen 1987, p. 1821, no. 58; Lecocq 2012, p. 194, no. 63; Dabin 1969, p. 102, no. 2.

[66] Vazeille 1834, p. 244, no. 568.

[67] Vazeille 1834, p. 244, no. 568.

possession. The monist theory of prescription entails that the usufruct continues to exist, as there is no possession. But Article 617 C.Nap. quite clearly says that usufruct is extinguished by non-use during thirty years (literally: "*le non-usage du droit pendant trente ans*").[68] If it were to say literally that usufruct is extinguished by extinctive prescription, there could be some wriggle room, as this would not necessarily exclude that the bare owner has to take back possession. But that is not what is said. Nowhere is it even merely implied that the bare owner has to take back possession.

In Dutch law, the monist theory of prescription does not meet this challenge. Mere non-use is insufficient to extinguish a limited real right. In addition to non-use, there has to be a situation which is contrary to the limited real right in question, against which the beneficiary of the limited real right has an action (Article 3:106 BW).[69] It is only the prescription of this action which extinguishes the limited real right. This strongly approaches a requirement for negative possession.

3.3.2. Instances of extinctive prescription that require possession

31. 'Possessory' extinctive prescription. Although in general no possession is required for extinctive prescription, there are some exceptions. These cases of extinctive prescription might be interpreted as an acknowledgment of the true monist nature of prescription. On the other hand, they also might just be necessitated by special circumstances.

32. Prescription of the *rei vindicatio*. In Belgian and French law, the *rei vindicatio* is considered unable to prescribe because property rights are perpetual.[70] German and Dutch law, on the other hand, allow extinctive prescription of the *rei vindicatio*.[71] Germany is not very interesting, as the extinction of the *rei vindicatio* has no impact whatsoever on the property right: the possessor does not acquire the property right, but neither does the owner lose it.[72] This makes it possible to durably separate property and possession, which is has been criticised because it is considered highly undesirable.[73]

68 Article 706 C.Nap., which regulates the extinctive prescription of servitudes, is written in the same way.

69 Muylle 2012, p. 103–104, no. 138; Mijnssen, van Velten and Bartels 2008, p. 249–250, no. 205; Bartels, van Mierlo and Ploeger 2013, p. 532–533, no. 538.

70 Sagaert 2005, p. 7, no. 9; Vanbelle 1994–1995, p. 36, no. 14; Van Oevelen 1987, p. 1780, no. 23; Muylle 2013–2014, p. 8, no. 17; Sagaert and Apers 2014, p. 6–7. On the history of this, see: Kanayama 1988, p. 733 et seq.
France: Article 2227 *Code civil français*; Chauviré 2013, P. 70, no. 109.

71 *Netherlands:* Article 3:309 BW (confirmed in Article 3:314, paragraph 2 BW). van Es 2011, p. 49.
Germany: §197, paragraph 1, no. 2 BGB. Kunze 2000, p. 234.

72 Honsell 2005, p. 19.

73 Honsell 2005, p. 19. There are other reasons to make the *rei vindicatio* imprescriptible: Kunze 2000, p. 235.

The Dutch situation was the same as in Germany and has been criticized in the same way.[74] In the new BW, the separation of property and possession is made impossible by Article 3:105 BW.[75] This is a very interesting article for the proponents of a monist theory. It contains an example of extinctive prescription (of the *rei vindicatio*), to which is joined an acquisition by the possessor without any acquisitive prescription.[76] It follows that this extinctive prescription needs possession[77] by a third party who is not the owner, and leads to the acquisition of a real right. But is it not better to consider Article 3:105 BW as an instance of acquisitive prescription, as it leads to an acquisition?[78] It would be a very strange case of acquisitive prescription. Article 3:105, first paragraph BW gives the property right to the person who possesses the good at the moment that the action to end his possession is extinguished by prescription. It is not required that the possessor possesses personally or through another person during 20 years (the normal time for extinctive prescription).[79] This is consistent with a case of extinctive prescription, which only takes into account that the owner has not exercised his *rei vindicatio* (or other action) within the allotted time. The second paragraph of Article 3:105 BW confirms this. The former possessor, who has lost his possession involuntarily before the 20 years have run, can bring an action to recover possession within the year of his losing possession. He will then be considered to be the possessor at the moment that the twenty years have run and acquire the ownership. This paragraph would be useless if the new possessor had to possess the good during 20 years.

33. Adverse possession (England). English law has, in general, no need for acquisitive prescription. "Possession by itself gives a good title against all the world, except someone having a better legal right to possession."[80] Only extinctive prescription has a role to play, that being of extinguishing the action to recover possession by someone who has a better right to it. This extinctive prescription is largely dependent on the possession by the one who wishes to defend himself against an action to recover possession, as the prescription time only starts to run "when the land is in the possession of some person in whose favour the period of limitation can run".[81] Prescription has no acquisitive element but only strengthens an already existing right.[82] Section 17 of the Limitation Act 1980 confirms this by stipulating that "at the expiration of the period prescribed by this Act for any person to bring an action to recover land […] the title of that person to the

74 Beekhoven van den Boezem 2001, p. 720, no. 5.

75 Jansen 2011, p. 1–2; Van Zeben, Du Pon and Olthof 1981, p. 416.

76 Van Zeben, Du Pon and Olthof 1981, p. 417; Jansen 2011, p. 11 e.v.; Vuye 1997, p. 474.

77 It has been proposed to make detentors also eligible for this acquisition by extinctive prescription: Beekhoven van den Boezem 2001, p. 723, no. 7.

78 Muylle 2012, p. 539, no. 770; Van Straaten 1992, 79.

79 Jansen 2011, p. 12–13.

80 Harpum 2000, p. 88, no. 3–118; Burn and Cartwright 2006, p. 28; Papandréou-Deterville 2004, p. 88, no. 118, 96, no. 131; Cartwright 2010, p. 395; Clarke and Kohler 2009, p. 489. See for moveables: Lurger and Faber 2011, p. 980, no. 24.

81 Limitation Act 1980, Sch 1, para 8.

82 Cartwright 2010, p. 395.

land shall be extinguished." No transfer of a title or of property (as far as English law knows this concept) is alluded to.

Acquisitive prescription is not fully absent from English law. Easements and *profits à prendre*[83] can be acquired by acquisitive prescription.[84] Remarkably, these rights cannot be extinguished by mere non-use.[85] Probably, a material obstacle (such as building a house over an easement of way) would lead to extinctive prescription on the ground of section 15 of the Limitations Act 1980. This closely resembles the way in which the Code Napoléon regulates the extinctive prescription of continuous servitudes. Another way in which easements and *profits à prendre* could disappear is by proprietary estoppel (somewhat comparable to *abus de droit/rechtsmisbruik* in the Continental law systems).[86] But proprietary estoppel is not dependent on the running of time and therefore cannot be seen as a form of prescription.[87]

34. Conclusion. We see that the required possession is merely incidental. The studied actions concern the recovery of land or other goods, and therefore cannot accrue as long as no one has taken possession of the land or other goods. There is no possible defendant. Also, if no one has possession, the owner can retake possession by himself.

3.4. Common effects: acquisition of a right?

35. Introduction. Traditionally, the acquisition[88] by prescription is restricted to acquisitive prescription. Extinctive prescription merely extinguishes a right without transferring it or creating a new right. But there are a few examples of extinctive prescription where another regime has been created. In Dutch law, one can think of Article 3:105 BW; this article has already been analysed *supra*.

36. *Caisse des dépôts et consignations*. The Belgian and French *Caisse des dépôts et consignations* is a kind of state bank, which is responsible for consignations of money and financial instruments in certain cases provided by law (e.g. consignation of payments to which one party is condemned by a judgement which is going to be appealed; consignation of monies on 'sleeping' bank accounts). The monies and financial instruments deposited by the *Caisse* can be attained by extinctive prescription.[89] This extinctive prescription effects a transfer of property in favour of the State.

83 Easements can be (very roughly) understood as the common law equivalent of servitudes. *Profits à prendre* are rights to take natural resources (such as wood) from the land of another.

84 Papandréou-Deterville 2004, p. 299–301, nos. 464–467.

85 Gray and Gray 2009, p. 683–684, nos. 5.2.92–93; Papandréou-Deterville 2004, p. 303, no. 471.

86 Gray and Gray 2009, p. 685, no. 5.2.96.

87 Gray and Gray 2009, p. 1198–1199, nos. 9.2.7–8.

88 Regardless of whether this acquisition consists in the transfer of a old right or the creation of a new one.

89 *Belgium:* Articles 25–26 KB 18 maart 1935 no. 150 tot samenschakeling van de wetten betreffende de inrichting en de werking van de Deposito- en Consignatiekas en tot aanbrenging van wijzigingen daarin krachtens de wet van 31 juli 1934, *BS*, 21 maart 1935, 1.778.
France: Article L518–24 Code monétaire et financier. Mignot 2009, no. 47.

37. Acquisitive prescription? Is this 'translative extinctive prescription' actually a form of acquisitive prescription? This seems doubtful. The final beneficiary in a case of extinctive prescription is not the same (legal) person as the one who can be said to possess the monies and financial instruments. In Belgian law, the *Caisse* is defined as a 'separate administration' whose patrimony is to be kept strictly distinct from the national treasury.[90] French law only differs in that there is no legal commandment to keep the patrimony of the *Caisse* strictly distinct.[91] At the very least, the patrimony of the *Caisse* is a special, separated patrimony, so the prescription should benefit this patrimony, not the patrimony of the State.

Additionally, there is no possession. As consignee, the *Caisse* is a detentor.[92] It therefore cannot possess, unless there has been an interversion in its 'title' which makes possession possible.

Interestingly, the translative character of this extinctive prescription is generally explained as the effect of a presumed or real abandonment of the goods, so that they have become *res nullius*.[93] It is therefore considered equitable that the State, as guardian of the public interest, receives these abandoned goods.

38. Conclusion. Obviously, there are some similarities between this translative extinctive prescription and acquisitive prescription, most notably the fact that both lead to an acquisition. Nevertheless, the dissimilarities are too important. The crucial problem is the lack of any possession by the beneficiary. The translative extinctive prescription cannot prove the monist theory.

4. General conclusion

39. Monist tendencies, but dualist victory. The monist theory of prescription explains a number of facts well, such as Article 2229 Code Napoléon and in general the monist structure of the Code Napoléon, the extinctive prescription of certain servitudes or the monist treatment in some codes. It also has support in the older law, most notably in the Parisian customary law. It nevertheless has a number of flaws. There is a group of extinctive prescriptions (e.g. of monies deposited with the *Caisse des dépôts et consignations*) which do not need any possession by the ultimate beneficiary and exclude

90 Article 4, first paragraph KB 18 maart 1935 no. 150 tot samenschakeling van de wetten betreffende de inrichting en de werking van de Deposito- en Consignatiekas en tot aanbrenging van wijzigingen daarin krachtens de wet van 31 juli 1934, *BS*, 21 maart 1935, 1.778. Vranckx, Coremans and Dujardin, p. 1.

91 See Article 518-2 Code monétaire et financier. Article 518-16 Code monétaire et financier implies that the patrimony of the *Caisse* is kept separate from the national treasury, as otherwise it would be pointless to let the *Caisse* pay a kind of dividends to the State.

92 *RPDB*, I, *v° Caisse des dépots et consignations*, p. 801, no. 40.

93 Vranckx, Coremans and Dujardin, p. 21-22; *RPDB*, I, *v° Caisse des dépots et consignations*, p. 801, no. 42.

any possibility of possession. It can also be doubted that the monist theory would be practically useful. A possession by the debtor ('negative possession') can easily become ambiguous when the debtor is rich or poor, as in those cases a creditor might abstain from demanding his payment. This would annihilate the usefulness of prescription, as it would become most unclear whether a debt has been extinguished by prescription.

This contrasts with the dualist theory. Generally, the legislators prefer this hypothesis, even if their laws are sometimes more ambiguous. One need only remember Bigot-Préameneu, one of the members of the committee which wrote the Code Napoléon, who was firmly dualist. The Code Napoléon itself is less clear. Its structure and some of its articles are clearly monist, but the rules on the extinctive prescription of limited real rights in most cases exclude possession as a requirement. The German BGB and in a lesser way the Dutch BW make a clear difference between both types of prescription, while the recent reform of the Code Napoléon in France has eliminated most, if not all elements favouring the monist theory. Legal doctrine is overwhelmingly in favour of the dualist theory. The dualist theory also does not risk to render prescription useless, as possession – and, more importantly, its vices – continue to be irrelevant (with some exceptions).

The preceding elements prove to our satisfaction that the prescription is dualist. The majority view may sometimes be in error, but not this time.

Bibliography

Aubry and Rau 1842
Aubry and Rau, *Cours de droit civil français par C.-S. Zachariae*, I, Brussels: Hauman, 1842.

Bartels, van Mierlo and Ploeger 2013
Bartels, S.E., van Mierlo, A.I.M. and Ploeger, H.D., *Algemeen goederenrecht* in *Mr. C. Assers Handleiding tot de beoefening van het Nederlands Burgerlijk Recht*, Deventer: Kluwer, 2013,

Baudry-Lacantinerie and Tissier 1924
Baudry-Lacantinerie, G. and Tissier, A., *Traité théorique et pratique de droit civil*, XXVIII, *De la prescription*, Paris: Sirey, 1924.

Beekhoven van den Boezem 2001
Beekhoven van den Boezem, F.E.J., 'Onroerende zaken en verjaring van de revindicatie', *WNPR*, 2001, 719–724.

Bouabdallah 2014
Bouabdallah, S., *La réception du modèle français en droit civil belge. Exemple d'un transfert de droit*, Brussels: Bruylant, 2014.

Burn and Cartwright 2006
Burn, E.H. and Cartwright, J., *Cheshire and Burn's Modern Law of Real Property*, Oxford: Oxford University Press, 2006.

Clarke and Kohler 2009
Clarke, A. and Kohler, P., *Property Law. Commentary and Materials*, Cambridge: Cambridge University Press, 2009.

Dalloz 1832
Dalloz, *Jurisprudence du XIXe siècle*, XXII, Brussels: Tarlier, 1832.

Cartwright 2010
Cartwright, J., 'Réformer le droit de la prescription français: une perspective anglaise' in J. Cartwright, S. Vogenauer and S. Whittaker (eds.), *Regards comparatistes sur l'avant-projet de réforme du droit des obligations et de la prescription*, Paris: Société de législation comparée, 2010, 387 et seq.

Charondas le Caron 1605
Charondas le Caron, L., *Coustume de la ville, prévosté et vicomté de Paris:* Paris: Chevalier, 1605.

Chauviré 2013
Chauviré, Ph., *L'acquisition dérivée de la propriété. Le transfert volontaire des biens*, Issy-les-Moulineaux: Librairie générale de droit et de jurisprudence, 2013.

Dabin 1969
Dabin, J., 'Sur l'adage 'Contra non valentem agere non currit praescriptio" (annotation under Cass. 2 januari 1969), *RCJB*, 1969, 93–107.

de Chabrol-Chaméane 1835
de Chabrol-Chaméane, G., *Dictionnaire de législation usuelle, contenant les notions du droit civil, commercial, criminel et administratif, précédée de la Constitution belge annotée par Isid. Plaisant*, I-II, Brussels: H. Tarlier, 1835.

de Fréminville 1845
de Fréminville, M., *Traité de la minorité et de la tutelle*, II, Clermont, Thibaud-Landriot, 1845.

de Fréminville 1848
de Fréminville, M., *Traité de l'organisation et de la compétence des cours d'appel en matière civile et disciplinaire*, II, Clermont-Ferrand, 1848.

Deffaux 1841
Deffaux, M., *Encyclopédie des huissiers*, IV, Paris: Cotillon, 1841.

Dekkers and Dirix 2005
Dekkers, R. and Dirix, E., *Handboek Burgerlijk Recht*, II, *Zakenrecht. Zekerheden. Verjaring*, Antwerp: Intersentia, 2005.

De Page and Dekkers 1952
De Page, H. and Dekkers, R., *Traité élémentaire de droit civil belge*, V, *Les principaux contrats usuels, Deuxième partie. Les biens. Première partie*, Brussels: Bruylant, 1952.

De Page and Dekkers 1953
De Page, H. and Dekkers, R., *Traité élémentaire de droit civil belge*, VI, *Les biens. Deuxième partie. Les sûretés. Première partie*, Brussels: Bruylant, 1953.

De Page and Dekkers 1957
De Page, H. and Dekkers, R., *Traité élémentaire de droit civil belge*, VII, *Les privilèges. Les hypothèques. La transcription. La prescription*, Brussels: Bruylant, 1957.

De Weggheleire 2013
De Weggheleire, J., 'Verkrijgende verjaring: detentie en titelomzetting (mis)begrepen?' (annotation under Court of Appeal of Ghent 4 february 2010), *RW*, 2013, 901–904.

Domat 1756
Domat, J., *Les lois civiles dans leur ordre naturel. Le droit public et legum delectus*, I, Paris: Savoye, 1756.

Dross 2013
Dross, W., 'Prescription acquisitive - Définitions et conditions', *JurisClasseur civil (art. 2258-2271)*, 2013.

Duplessis 1727
Duplessis, C., 'Traité des prescriptions' in *Oeuvres*, II, Paris: Gosselin, 1728, 217 et seq.

Fenet 1836
Fenet, F.A., *Recueil complet des travaux préparatoires du Code civil*, XV, Paris: Videcocq, 1836.

Gray and Gray 2009
Gray, K. and Gray, S.F., *Elements of Land Law*, Oxford: Oxford University Press, 2009.

Hansenne 1983
Hansenne, J., 'La prescription acquisitive' in *Rép.not.*, II, *Les biens*, VII, 1983.

Harpum 2000
Harpum, Ch., *Magarry & Wade. The Law of Real Property*, Londen, Sweet & Maxwell, 2000.

Hevin, d'Argentré and Du Moulin 1746
Hevin, P., d'Argentré, B. and Du Moulin, Ch., *Coûtumes générales du païs et duché de Bretagne et usemens locaux de la mesme province*, II, Rennes, Vatar, 1746.

Honsell 2005
Honsell, H., 'Einleitung zum BGB' in *Staudinger BGB. Eckpfeiler des Zivilrechts*, Berlin: de Gruyter, 2005, 1 et seq.

Jansen 2011
Jansen, J.E., *Bezit te kwader trouw, verkrijgende en bevrijdende verjaring. Een leerstellige rechtsvergelijkende studie op historische grondslag*, Den Haag: Boom Juridische uitgevers, 2011.

Jourdain 1995
Jourdain, P., *Les biens*, Paris: Dalloz, 1995.

Kanayama 1988
Kanayama, N., 'La révolution et la prescription: La naissance du principe de l'imprescriptibilité de l'action en revendication en droit français' in J. Bart et al. (eds.), *La révolution et l'ordre juridique privé. Rationalité ou scandale?*, II, Paris: PUF, 1988, 733 et seq.

Kunze 2000
Kunze, H.H., *Restitution "entarteter Kunst". Sachenrecht und Internationales Privatrecht*, Berlin: de Gruyter, 2000.

Lecocq 2003
Lecocq, P., 'De la prescription acquisitive abrégée: autour et alentour du juste titre' (annotation under Cass. 7 september 2001), *RCJB*, 2003, 428–455.

Le Roux de Bretagne 1869
Le Roux de Bretagne, A., *Nouveau traité de la prescription en matière civile*, II, Paris: Durand en Pedone-Lauriel, 1869.

Laurent 1878
Laurent, F., *Principes de droit civil français*, XXXII, Brussels: Bruylant, 1878.

Lecocq 2012
Lecocq, P., *Manuel de droit des biens*, I, *Biens et propriété*, Brussels: Larcier, 2012.

Lurger and Faber 2011
Lurger, B. and Faber, W., *Acquisition and Loss of Ownership of Goods. Principles of European Law*, München: Sellier, 2011.

Merlin de Douai 1813
Merlin de Douai, Ph.A., *Répertoire universel et raisonné de jurisprudence*, IX, *Pac - Prise*, Paris: Garnery, 1813.

Merlin de Douai 1827
Merlin de Douai, Ph.-A., *Répertoire universel et raisonné de jurisprudence*, XXI, *Mou - Ocl*, Brussels: Tarlier, 1827, *v° prescription*, 65 et seq.

Martin 1972
Martin, O., *Histoire de la coutume de la prévôté et vicomté de Paris:* II, Paris: Éditions Cujas, 1972.

Masschelein 2010
Masschelein, M.A., *Het verval van een recht in het materieel privaatrecht. La déchéance*, Antwerp: Intersentia, 2010.

Mignot 2009
Mignot, M., 'Prescription extinctive - Dispositions générales', *JurisClasseur civil*, 2009.

Mijnssen, van Velten and Bartels 2008
Mijnssen, F.H.J., van Velten, A.A. and Bartels, S.E., *Zakenrecht. Eigendom en beperkte rechten* in *Mr. C. Assers Handleiding tot de beoefening van het Nederlands Burgerlijk Recht*, Deventer: Kluwer, 2008.

Muylle 2012
M. Muylle, *De duur en de beëindiging van zakelijke rechten*, Antwerp: Intersentia, 2012.

Muylle 2013–2014
Muylle, M., 'Het eeuwigdurend karakter van het eigendomsrecht. Oude materie, nieuwe perspectieven', *RW*, 2013–14, 4–16.

Papandréou-Deterville 2004
Papandréou-Deterville, M.-F., *Le droit anglais des biens*, Paris: LGDJ, 2004.

Pothier 1825
Pothier, R.J., 'Traité de la prescription qui résulte de la possession' in M. Dupin (ed.), *Œuvres de Pothier, contenant les traités du droit français*, VIII, Paris: Béchet, 1825, 389 et seq.

Poullain du Parc 1769
Poullain du Parc, A.-M., *Principes du droit françois, suivant les maximes de Bretagne*, VI, Rennes, Vatar, 1769.

Rutten 2011
Rutten, S., *De betaling. Juridische aard en rechtsgevolgen*, Antwerp: Intersentia, 2011.

Sagaert 2005
Sagaert, V., 'Het onderscheid tussen persoonlijke en zakelijke vorderingen – Het verjaringsregime van zakelijke vorderingen nader geanalyseerd' in I. Claeys (ed.), *Verjaring in het privaatrecht. Weet de avond wat de morgen brengt?*, Malines: Kluwer, 2005, 1 et seq.

Sagaert 2012–2013
Sagaert, V., 'Over de hoogte van erfdienstbaarheden' (annotation under Rb. Tongeren 14 november 2011), *RW*, 2012–13, 1473–1475.

Sagaert 2014
Sagaert, V., *Goederenrecht* in *Beginselen van Belgisch Privaatrecht*, Malines: Kluwer, 2014.

Sagaert and Apers 2014
Sagaert, V. and Apers, A., 'Kroniek privaat vastgoedrecht (2010–2013)' in V. Sagaert (ed.), *Themis. Vastgoedrecht*, Bruges: die Keure, 2014, 1 et seq.

Seresia 1873
Seresia, A., *De la pétition d'hérédité en droit moderne*, Brussels: Bruylant, 1873.

Storme 2000
Storme, M.E., 'De drievoudige gelaagdheid van schuldvorderingen en hun bescherming' in *Liber Amicorum Walter van Gerven*, Deurne, Kluwer, 2000, 329 et seq.

van Es 2011
van Es, P.C., *Verkrijging door verjaring*, Nijmegen: Ars Aequi Libri, 2011.

Vanbelle 1994–1995
Vanbelle, J., 'De revindicatie van onroerende en roerende goederen', *Jura Falc.*, 1994-1995, 31–62.

Verjans 2014
Verjans, E., 'Correctiefiguren op de onbillijke gevolgen van de bevrijdende verjaring', *TBBR*, 2014, 146–166.

Vranckx, Coremans and Dujardin
Vranckx, A.W., Coremans, H. and Dujardin, J., *Deposito- en Consignatiekas* in *Administratief Lexicon*, Bruges: die Keure, *s.d.*

Willems 2011
Willems, K., *De natuurlijke verbintenis*, Bruges: die Keure, 2011.

Van Straaten 1992
Van Straaten, J.C., *Kadaster, openbare registers en derdenbescherming*, Deventer, Kluwer, 1992.

Van Zeben, Du Pon and Olthof 1981
Van Zeben, C.J., Du Pon, J.W. and Olthof, M.M. (eds.), *Parlementaire geschiedenis van het nieuwe Burgerlijk Wetboek. Boek 3. Vermogensrecht in het algemeen*, Deventer: Kluwer, 1981.

Van Drooghenbroeck and Marchandise 2010
Van Drooghenbroeck, J.-Fr. and Marchandise, M., 'Les causes d'interruption et de suspension de la prescription libératoire. Rapport belge' in P. Jourdain and P. Wéry (eds.), *La prescription extinctive. Études de droit comparé*, Brussels: Bruylant, 2010, 403 et seq.

Van Oevelen 1987
Van Oevelen, A., 'Algemeen overzicht van de bevrijdende verjaring en de vervaltermijnen in het Belgisch privaatrecht', *TPR*, 1987, 1755–1842.

Van Oevelen 2000–2001
Van Oevelen, A., 'Recente ontwikkelingen inzake de bevrijdende verjaring in het burgerlijk recht', *RW*, 2000–2001, 1433–1444.

Vazeille 1824
Vazeille, F.A., *Traité des prescriptions*, Paris: Bavoux, 1824.

Vazeille 1834
Vazeille, F.A., *Traité des prescriptions. Edition augmentée et mise en rapport, par notes, avec la législation et la jurisprudence de Belgique*, Brussels: Tarlier, 1834.

Vuye 1994
Vuye, H., *Bezit en bezitsbescherming van onroerende goederen en onroerende rechten*, Bruges: die Keure, 1994.

Vuye 1997
Vuye, H., 'Une autre approche de la possession? Esquisse de la possession et de la protection possessoire dans le (nouveau) Code civil des Pays-Bas', *TBBR*, 1997, 453–476.

Vuye 2003
Vuye, H., 'Possession et actions possessoires: Belgique, Pays-bas et France. A la recherche d'un ius commune?', *ERPL*, 2003, 321–341.

Wintgen 2010
Wintgen, R., 'La réforme du droit français de la prescription: perspective française' in J. Cartwright, S. Vogenauer and S. Whittaker (eds.), *Regards comparatistes sur l'avant-projet de réforme du droit des obligations et de la prescription*, Paris: Société de législation comparée, 2010, 375 et seq.

Zenati and Fournier 1996
Zenati, F. and Fournier, S., 'Essai d'une théorie unitaire de la prescription', *RTD civ.*, 1996, 339–353.

IUS COMMUNE EUROPAEUM

A peer-reviewed book series in which the common foundations of the legal systems of the Member States of the European Union are the central focus.

The *Ius Commune Europaeum* series includes horizontal comparative legal studies as well as studies on the effect of treaties within the national legal systems. All the classic fields of law are covered. The books are published in various European languages under the auspices of METRO, the Institute for Transnational Legal Research at Maastricht University.

Recently published:
Volume 131: *State Aid and Public Procurement in the European Union*, S. Schoenmaekers, W. Devroe and N. Philipsen (eds.)
Volume 132: *Property Law Perspectives III*, A. Apers, S. Bouly et al. (eds.)
Volume 133: *Multi-Party Redress Mechanisms in Europe: Squeaking Mice?*, V. Harsági and C.H. van Rhee (eds.)
Volume 134: *Europe at the Edge of Pluralism*, D. Gozdecka and M. Kmak
Volume 135: *Cooperative Agreements between Public Authorities. The Influence of CJEU Case Law on National Legal Systems*, K. Wauters
Volume 136: *Common Core, PECL and DCFR: Could They Change Shipping and Transport Law?*, W. Verheyen, F.G.M. Smeele and M.A.I.H. Hoeks
Volume 137: *Who does What? On the Allocation of Competences in European Private Law*, B. Akkermans, J. Hage, N. Kornet and J.M. Smits
Volume 138: *The Nature of Mutual Recognition in European Law.* W. van Ballegooij
Volume 139: *Evidence in Contemporary Civil Procedure. Fundamental Issues in a Comparative Perspective*, C.H. van Rhee and A. Uzelac (eds.)
Volume 140: *The effect of D&O insurance on managerial risk taking*, Max Gaber
Volume 141: *Information and Notification Duties*, Ilse Samoy and Marco B. Loos
Volume 142: *The Application of the Theory of Efficient Breach in Contract Law. A Comparative Law and Economics Perspective*, Wenqing Liao
Volume 143: *A European Legal Framework for Nuclear Liability. Rethinking Current Approaches*, Tobias Heldt
Volume 144: *The Development of European Private Law in a Multi-Level Legal Order*, Esther A.G. van Schagen

www.ingramcontent.com/pod-product-compliance
Ingram Content Group UK Ltd.
Pitfield, Milton Keynes, MK11 3LW, UK
UKHW051928100926
8556IPUK00022B/1434

9 781780 68370